Lucy Moore is the founder of Messy Chur~' ~-growing
ministry that is now in over 20 co~~ romotes
Messy Church nationally ~ ng and
speaking events, and le *The*
Gospels Unplugged (Bar ~rship
(BRF, 2010).

Messy Church is a fast-grow ~ ~~nistry that continues to engage and
build relationships with thousands of people outside the usual church
context. Week by week we are seeing new Messy Churches starting
across the UK, as well as in other countries around the world.

Messy Church is resourced, supported and enabled by BRF as one
of its core ministries. It is largely funded by grants and donations.
We need your help to continue to enable the growth and ongoing
development of Messy Churches, large and small, wherever they are
found.

Could you or your church help BRF's Messy Church ministry
continue to make a difference through giving and prayer? www.
messychurch.org.uk/support-messy-church.

Messy Church® is a registered word mark and the logo is a registered device mark of The Bible Reading Fellowship

Text copyright © Lucy Moore 2012
The author asserts the moral right
to be identified as the author of this work

Published by
The Bible Reading Fellowship
15 The Chambers, Vineyard
Abingdon OX14 3FE, United Kingdom
Tel: +44 (0)1865 319700
Email: enquiries@brf.org.uk
Website: www.brf.org.uk
BRF is a Registered Charity

ISBN 978 0 85746 120 9
First published 2012
Reprinted 2012, 2013, 2014, 2015
10 9 8 7 6 5 4
All rights reserved

Acknowledgments
Story on page 54 adapted from an original idea in *Good, Better, Best: The story of Mary and Martha*, Marilyn Lashbrook (Lion Hudson, 2007).

Take-home ideas on pages 57, 75, 85, 117, 126, 147 and 156 taken from www.faithinhomes.org.uk.

Take-home idea on page 94 taken from www.faithinhomes.org.uk, adapted from *The Lord's Prayer Unplugged* (Barnabas for Children, 2012).

Story on page 64 abbreviated from Martyn Payne's story on www.barnabasinchurches.org.uk, inspired by Godly Play™.

Unless otherwise stated, scripture quotations are taken from the Holy Bible, Today's New International Version®. Copyright © 2001, 2005 by Biblica®. Used by permission of Biblica®. All rights reserved worldwide. 'TNIV' and 'Today's New International Version' are trademarks registered in the United States Patent and Trademark Office by Biblica®. Use of either trademark requires the permission of Biblica.

Page 126: scripture quotation taken from the Contemporary English Version of the Bible, published by HarperCollins Publishers, copyright © 1991, 1992, 1995 American Bible Society.

Cover background image: istockphoto/© Peter Zelei

Every effort has been made to trace and contact copyright owners for material used in this resource. We apologise for any inadvertent omissions or errors, and would ask those concerned to contact us so that full acknowledgment can be made in the future.

A catalogue record for this book is available from the British Library

Printed and bound by CPI Group (UK) Ltd, Croydon, CR0 4YY

Fifteen sessions for exploring the Christian life with families

MESSY CHURCH 3

Lucy Moore

For Judith, brightest, best, most beautiful (and messiest)
of daughters, with love

ACKNOWLEDGMENTS

I owe a huge debt, as ever, to the teams at BRF and in St Wilf's Messy Church in Cowplain, which is enjoying getting messier than ever. My colleague Jane Leadbetter has contributed hugely to this book, and Martyn Payne has allowed me to mess around with ideas from the www.barnabasinchurches.org.uk website. Jane Butcher has been the source of many of the take-home ideas from the ever-fruitful www. faithinhomes.org.uk website. Lesley Baker devised the celebration on Martha and Mary, and Paul Moore came up with the celebrations for Easter and Christmas. Thanks, too, to Beth Barnett for her inspiring thoughts about Paul and childhood. The St Wilf's team in Cowplain and L19:Messy Church in Liverpool have kindly field-tested ideas and poured helpful scorn and derision on ideas that would otherwise have wasted your time with their unworkableness. Thank you especially to Pete, Kate, Elisabeth and Denise for your diplomatic suggestions, and my apologies for the ideas that got through the net despite your best efforts. Thanks, too, to the other Messy Church groups who have been given different sessions to field-test throughout the year.

Contents

Foreword

Rapidly growing in a remarkably short space of time from one small church in Portsmouth, UK, to over 1000 registered Messy Church expressions around the world, the story of Messy Church is an amazing one. Arising from the God-given imagination of one person, Messy Church has captured the imagination of a diverse range of individuals, congregations and denominations across the globe. Many communities of faith have been and continue to be blessed, challenged and served through Messy Church as they bless, challenge and serve their local communities through their uniquely contextualised expression of Messy Church.

One of the many blessings of Messy Church for local congregations has been a re-energising and re-commitment to multi-age engagement. Arguably one of the significant shifts taking place in ministry with children and their families is a move away from an individualist, isolated or segregated approach back to a community-oriented, integrated and inclusive model. In many ways Messy Church can be seen as both reflecting this trend and furthering the momentum of this welcome change.

In terms of challenge, a decision to explore Messy Church has prompted many local congregations to reflect upon their identity as 'church' (a somewhat inward focus) and re-think their engagement with local communities (an outward focus). A positive outcome of this, in many situations, has been a reconnecting of local congregations with their local community. Stories abound, too, of children and grandchildren of church participants reconnecting with a local congregation through Messy Church.

In addition to providing wonderful resources, *Messy Church 3* creatively addresses many of the questions that arise when churches embark upon the Messy Church adventure. Drawing not just on the experience of Messy Church, but the wisdom of others such as George Lings, Paul Moore and Keith White, *Messy Church 3* is an invaluable addition to the ever-growing list of Messy Church resources. May Messy Church continue to bless, challenge and serve local congregations as they seek to participate more fully in the ministry of Christ in the world.

Chris Barnett, Centre for Theology and Ministry, Uniting Church in Australia

Introduction

Hello, Messy Church leaders! It's strange to think that when I wrote *Messy Church* in 2006 there were only a few people running Messy Churches. Now there are hundreds of us from different denominations and countries: all very good fun and more than a little mind-blowing. God is doing something very exciting for families and churches in our generation and it's a joy to be a tiny part of it.

I felt rather hesitant about writing the Messy Church sessions in this book, as there are so many people creating their own marvellous and inventive sessions month by month who won't need this book in the slightest—except to have the satisfaction of grunting, 'Hmmph. Our ideas are *much* better than these!' Which is just as it should be. But for those who email us in search of fresh ideas, I hope this will at least give a starting point for another year or so of Messy Church for the families where you are.

In this book you'll find 15 sessions for Messy Church that are, in the great Messy tradition, suggestions for you to adapt and improve for your own circumstances, rather than an inflexible programme to be adhered to. The reasoning behind the choice of themes comes from several sources.

The first is experience. It may look more constructive to have a series that extends over several months, but in practice, most people find it hard to hold the narrative thread across a month's gap, so a series isn't necessarily very helpful and can be restrictive. Instead, we've taken the Christian year as a whole, offering one-off sessions, which nevertheless have themes that link them. We also felt it was helpful to start offering 'tools' of faith, like the Lord's Prayer—so that prayer features throughout. And as we've got to know the families coming to Messy Church, we've tried to be more sensitive about themes that will engage them. So experience has helped us shape these sessions, and the three spoof letters that make up the final part of the introduction contain more experiences that may be helpful to your own situation.

The second source is Paul Moore's research on discipleship in Messy Church (see *Making Disciples in Messy Church*, BRF, 2013), where he advises that:

> Messy Church should develop an intentional socialisation programme of imaginative, participative all-age celebrations at major festivals of the Christian calendar. God's people thereby learn to live in a rhythm of reviewing, renewing and passing on their faith. Alongside this we need to help people to develop a weekly Sabbath rhythm and also the vital heartbeat of faith being worked out together in the family home and in all aspects of life throughout the week.

So the sessions have a focus on the Christian year: Christmas, Easter, Pentecost and Harvest, with a nod to Rogationtide (a festival that is rarely celebrated these days, and falls just before Ascension Day) and All Saints' Day. These festivals help us to establish key points of the Christian faith: God's creation and ongoing care for the world (a theme also recognised in Session 14: 'Pets and Peace'); Christ's birth, death and resurrection; and the coming of the Holy Spirit. They also give us a chance to reflect on prayer (Session 6: 'The Lord's Prayer') and on the Bible (Session 10: 'Light up the darkness', or the 'non-Hallowe'en-but-still-lots-of-fun-dressing-up-and-doing-wacky-things' session).

The festivals are like a 'Christian basics' course that we follow every year, building a dependable pattern in a transient, shifting society. But the world we live and move in has other festivals that, although not exclusively church festivals, are important to us, and I've included some of these as they reinforce excellent Christian values. Since these may not be at the same times of year across the different countries in which Messy Church happens, I've tried to keep them as focused as possible on the theme rather than the season:

✣ Mothering Sunday (or Mother's Day as it is now more commonly known) and Father's Day give us a chance to think about the family of the church, to be grateful to those who parent us and to celebrate the parenting of God, whom Jesus called 'Father'.

✛ Valentine's Day is about that value at the heart of our faith—love.
✛ Remembrance Day is about service, sacrifice and gratitude.

Another source I've drawn on is Keith White's book, *The Growth of Love* (Barnabas for Children, 2011), in which he describes five essential elements for child development and the growth of love. It seems to me that these are not exclusive to the growth of love in children but can be a useful basis for growing love in adults too. So the sessions reinforce the ideas of

✛ security: that we are loved unconditionally;
✛ boundaries: that there are wholesome guidelines within which to live our family lives;
✛ significance: that we matter to others and to God;
✛ community: that we are connected and not alone;
✛ creativity, which of course underpins everything in Messy Church.

While these are implicit in many of the themes of the sessions, there is logic in having a session about forgiveness (Session 1: 'A new start'), a session about celebrating our own community (Session 7: 'Our community') and a session to expand that concept of community (Session 8: 'Journeys').

A further source, *The 8 Secrets of Happiness* (Paul Griffiths and Martin Robinson, Lion Hudson, 2009) provides guidance for some of the emphases in the sessions. If Christianity is about transforming lives, there are worse places to start than trying to make a difference to the lives of families in the UK. The church is the perfect place to make opportunities for families to be happy, and to change the gloom level of a nation. So the eight secrets of happiness are to

✛ count your blessings;
✛ practise acts of kindness;
✛ savour life's joys;
✛ thank a mentor;
✛ learn to forgive;

✤ invest time and energy in friends and family;
✤ take care of your body and soul;
✤ develop strategies for coping with stress and hardships.

These provide a backdrop to all the sessions, and come to the fore in Session 11: 'Money matters' and in Session 15: 'Healthy body, healthy soul'.

Without wanting to overwhelm overstretched Messy Church leaders, I have included some ideas for building on the opportunities we have been given in Messy Church to go that little bit further with families who are keen to explore faith.

Sunday treat

This picks up on the idea of reviving interest in a Sabbath rhythm and suggests a simple prayer for families to pray together on Sundays during the month. These short, imaginative prayers are based on the Lord's Prayer, the Grace, the Trinity and the simple phrase 'world without end'. They invite families to add their own words and ideas, and so will be different every Sunday. The Sunday treats could be included on a Facebook page or in a weekly text to your families; they might provide an excuse to drop round and visit your families; they could be printed out on cards and decorated at Messy Church or beforehand; or they could go on the handout sheet.

Take-home ideas

Many of us are already sending ideas home at the end of each Messy Church. These send out the message that church isn't just about coming together once a month; it's about living out our faith in our homes, schools and workplaces every day of the month. It also helps carers and parents become aware that it's their job to guide their children in faith, rather than leaving it up to the church. I've only suggested one per month in the hope that churches will think of even better ideas, making use of the www.faithinhomes.org.uk website and encouraging their families on to this and similar websites. The ideas aren't just about growing up in God; they're about growing closer as a family too.

Messy team theme

This is provided because many of us see Messy Church as a fantastic way to grow the group of disciples that make up the team itself. Gathering together once a month with something nice to eat and drink and discussing a few simple questions gives energy and purpose to the team. The topics covered are based on the themes of the actual sessions; you could discuss the ones for the session you're about to run as preparation for it.

Songs

I haven't included song suggestions in this book as people's tastes, musicianship and access to technology or performers vary so greatly, but look out for suggestions on the Messy Church website.

Meals

Again, every team has its own ideas about food by now and, as *Messy Cooks* (BRF, 2011) contains a wide variety of menus, and many Messy Churches stick to one or two recipes for very good reasons, there is no point in duplicating those recipes here. I hope everyone has seen by now what a crucial part the meal has to play in a Messy Church community and how important it is not to be tempted to miss it out.

And the future? Will we go on with *Messy Church 4... 5... 6*? Not unless there's a very good reason. Watch out instead for *Get Messy!*, a three-times-a-year subscription magazine, which will be the next regular resource from BRF. It will contain a Messy Church session for each month, plus Bible studies, up-to-date stories, reflections and reports. It will appear on your doormat in plenty of time to plan the next season of Messy Church with your team. Even better, it will be written by Messy Church leaders of different denominations, backgrounds, areas and ages, so *Get Messy!* will draw on experiences from a far wider team and give a great pool of expertise for us all to benefit from as we keep on growing God's kingdom in the churches where he's placed us. Exciting stuff!

A LETTER TO THE CHURCHES IN CLODPOOL-IN-THE-MARSH SOME TIME AGO

Dear Helen, Revd Higgins and Pastor Percy

Thanks so much for your long and detailed letter asking about starting a Messy Church. It must have taken you a very long time to write, and something about the heavy crossings-out, the crumpled state of page 37 and indeed the splatters of blood on the paper indicate a certain degree of tension between you as you grapple with the best way forward for your community. But I'm sure this can be resolved in true Christian amity without further violence.

You ask for a summary of what Messy Church actually is. It's a way of being church that is for all ages, on a day and at a time that suits families in your area. It usually involves a welcome; a time of making things on a biblical theme; a celebration on the same theme with story, song and prayer; and a meal around tables for everyone. Its values are being all-age, being Christ-centred, hospitality, creativity and celebration. It started in 2004 in the Anglican church of St Wilfrid's in Cowplain near Portsmouth in the UK, comes under the wing of BRF, the Bible Reading Fellowship, and has since spread across all the major Christian denominations and around the world to at least thirteen countries. By the end of 2011 there were over 1000 different Messy Churches listed on the Messy Church online directory. So much for the bare bones.

You ask about the practicalities of starting a Messy Church: 'We find ourselves unable to agree whether to start this month or to spend the next two years in prayer and meditation, seeking guidance before we visit the local Hobbycraft store.' You'll find the book *Starting*

Your Messy Church (BRF, 2012) very helpful, I think: it is short and to the point. There's also oodles of help and advice on the Messy Church website (www.messychurch.org.uk), along with templates for the documents you might want to use: registration forms; feedback forms; planning sheets; questions to ask when you visit another Messy Church; and advice on child protection, food hygiene and the like.

In terms of how long you should pray for—well, it's impossible to set a time sheet for God, and steeping yourselves in prayer beforehand is indeed the best possible foundation for your plans. At the same time, after you've spent two years in prayer, the children who are eight now will be ten years old... then twelve... then fourteen... and before we know it, another generation will have missed out on the chance to enjoy church with their family and friends. Some churches report finding a *kairos* moment to start their Messy Churches, a moment that is in God's timing, not ours. They try at one point and the project has no energy, drive, vision or support; they try again some time later and things slot into place effortlessly. You might pray that you find your *kairos* moment.

You say that your team has visited three local Messy Churches and found that each of them is slightly different:

> Helen said that the one she saw had only three craft activities. Wilberforce has denounced the one he visited as heresy: it was not on a Thursday afternoon, did not start at 3.30pm and did not follow the prescribed liturgy as laid out in the book *Messy Church*. And Dwayne discovered that the one he attended on a Sunday afternoon served sandwiches and soup instead of a full cooked meal. After we had argued for two hours in the Spotted Pig about what constitutes a true Messy Church, we sat glumly round our pints feeling that we no longer knew what any church is.

Yes, it makes me ask what church is too. You'll be relieved to know that Messy Church is less of a rigid model to follow religiously than a suggested pattern that has proved useful to many. But the pattern needs adapting to your own context so that it's right for the people around you. If you're in a sparsely populated village, or have only a short time available, you might find that a smaller number of activities is more suitable than the ten suggested in the book. Thursday happens to be a good day for us; Saturday or Monday might be better for you. And the order of events, or the nature of the meal provided, doesn't matter in the slightest. The appeal to all ages does; the Christ-centredness of everything does, as do the warm welcome, emphasis on creativity and celebration, and the inclusion of a meal. You are the experts on your area and will want to adapt the shape and details to suit your people, while guarding the tried-and-tested principles behind Messy Church. It's not a prescribed programme but a set of values that gives your creativity and imagination a chance to work to the glory of God in the place where you live.

There were one or two other issues about Messy Church that I picked up from your letter, which I'll address, if I may. You say, 'Can you suggest a different name? We've decided not to call it Messy Church as Mrs Penworthy-Smythe, a member of one of our churches, finds the word "messy" offensive, and threatens to leave the church if we call it by such a disrespectful and irreverent name.' You can call it whatever you like, of course, and if it has the same values as Messy Church and follows a similar pattern, there's nothing stopping you registering it on the online directory, whatever it's called. But I would urge you to consider carefully before you call it something different. You might be throwing out the gravy with the giblets. I hate to say it as it sounds so crass and consumerist, but Messy Church is a recognised brand and, as such, we could either wring our hands in horror at such commercialism or try to make the most of this fact. As there are now so many Messy Churches, it is already something that people trust. People move house and email us looking for another Messy Church in their new community. The anecdotal evidence is that people gossip about how much they enjoy Messy Church, so you could benefit from that news-spreading. By using the name you can make the most of the international network of generous supporters and friends who also run Messy Churches. You'd have a ready-made logo free to download and use on your publicity materials, as well as a range of professionally produced craft items, mugs, T-shirts, posters, stickers and so on that you can easily obtain from the companies we work with.

I also think there's a big difference between giving this enterprise a different name because it works better for the people you're trying to reach, and calling it something different because a church member doesn't like it. Mrs P-S is already a member of the church: Messy Church isn't there primarily to help her grow in Christ, although that may be one of its side effects. In mission, the preferences of believers have to give way to the needs of unbelievers. The apostle Paul wrote, 'I have become all things to all people so that by all possible means I might save some' (1 Corinthians 9:22). I expect that wasn't always comfortable for him either.

It might help to explain to Mrs P-S that 'messy' refers to the liquid edges of church membership where people feel neither in nor out; it is about how God loves to work with people whose lives are in a mess, and the unpredictable way he takes us on adventures with him. But then again, she might be even more horrified at the thought that God might actually want to change things. It's probably best just to say you think the name's fun and plan to try it out for a six-month pilot period.

You describe your plans for 'a lovely messy club for the kiddies to have a nice time… a bridge into proper church on a Sunday so that we can restart our Sunday school and it can be as thriving as it was when we were young… a way of hooking the parents…' It's a crucial foundational idea of Messy Church that it is for all ages, not just for children. It makes my heart ache when I hear of Messy Churches where only the children are encouraged to do the crafts, or where the adults are excluded, implicitly or explicitly, from the celebration, or where there is only food for the under-fives. How do we learn best? By having models around us, living it out for us, showing us what to do and more importantly how to do it. If children see that the adults don't take part, doesn't this mean that the message you're sending out is 'creativity is just for children', or 'only under-elevens need to sit round a table to eat' or 'grown-ups don't worship'? In other words, 'You'll grow out of it.' Are you depriving adults of a chance to meet a God who longs for them to know him as much as he longs for their children to know him? Messy Church isn't about attempting to attract the children so that their parents are 'hooked'. It's about being a transparent, honest, messy household of faith together, learning from and with each other so that our lost generations have the opportunity to encounter a living Lord and grow in faith with us.

And, forgive me, but is it really about starting 'a bridge to proper church'? Is it just a stepping-stone to the once-weekly service, which has a style and language and reflects attitudes that long-time believers have grown accustomed to? Although this has value, it may not be the best way for the old and young who are just dipping a toe in the water of church-going to feel the attraction, relevance, mystery and fun that make up church. I was clumsily expressing something of this once at a training event in Herefordshire, when a grumpy-looking elderly minister interrupted, 'But who says we've got it right on Sundays anyway? Why do we assume *that's* the best or only way of being church?'

If the Sunday school is no more, maybe God is bringing something new to birth, not trying to artificially resuscitate something that has done a wonderful job in its time. The Sunday school has served its purpose and gracefully died—just as I expect Messy Church will one day die to make space for God's next even-more inventive idea to pour out his love on people. 'There is a time for everything, and a season for every activity under the heavens: a time to be born and a time to die' (Ecclesiastes 3:1–2). Try treating your Messy Church as a congregation that is just as important as other congregations, such as the early-morning Eucharist—it will take on a very different dimension from just being a 'club'. It will matter if it starts going wrong or when God works wonders in it.

You also mention the team you're putting together. 'We find ourselves unable to agree on the proper statement of faith for the helpers to sign before they are permitted to help, and attach the proposed 16-page document for your approval.' I've taken the liberty of putting this in the recycling bin. This is messy leadership: you need to get messy people on board. You need people whose lives aren't perfect; people who aren't certain what they believe about every aspect of life and faith; people whose families are busy making as many mistakes as ours and who aren't ashamed to say it; people who are simply responding to God's call to serve his people and who are ready to grow in him along the way. You need older people who can show you what it means to have a love of God at the end of this life. You need younger people who will galvanise you with their ideas and attitudes. You need everyone in between: people with disabilities, women, teenagers, men, people of every colour, single people, married people, children, parents and grandparents to be the scintillating mosaic of community around the people who come. Let God worry about the purity of their beliefs and about the exemplary nature of their lifestyle. He can sort that out along the way as each member of the team encounters him, grapples with the Bible stories you're exploring and works out how to respond to the questions that come their way through their mission and evangelism.

A Messy Church team is work in progress. And that will be messy, just as an artist's studio is messy. Your job is to notice the God-moments for them as well as for the families who come, and to help the team members to build on every opportunity God gives them. One Messy Church I visited had to deal with a physical fight between two mums. Two years later one of the mums was on the leadership team. Give God a chance and he will work miracles.

You describe in veiled terms the scene that ensued when the treasurers of the three churches came together. I can only say I wish I had been there to witness it too. And you say:

> Horace Ramsbotham, treasurer of The Church of the Wild 'n' Free, refused to believe there is no charge for starting a Messy Church and has insisted on seeing in print that registering a Messy Church on the directory will not, emphatically not, incur a series of annual charges

for the use of the name. We persuaded him to step down from the table top only after we had promised to ask you to confirm this.

OK, this is how it works from the BRF end. We took the decision, very early on in the development of Messy Church, that, since this was a ministry that God had, for some reason, entrusted to BRF, we wanted it to be freely available to churches to help the kingdom grow. So we would make no charge for using the idea, the name or the logo. We rely for help on the generosity of charitable trusts and individuals who have caught the vision for the way God is transforming people and churches through Messy Church. If Messy Church is valuable to your churches, we would love you to consider contributing a gift to the core costs of the ministry through the Messy Champions scheme, in the same way as your church no doubt contributes to other mission societies or charities to grow the kingdom. But please assure Mr Ramsbotham that we will never demand payment. We would simply ask that he considers whether it would be money well spent to help keep the centre of Messy Church in a healthy financial state.

I have left until last to say how excellent it is that you are considering starting up a Messy Church jointly. Despite your obvious disagreements, and however hard you find it to get on with each other personally, you are all passionately committed to working together on the principle of putting your community's needs before the needs of the individual churches. This is brilliant. People outside the church don't give a green teacup for the denomination of their local church— it's 'the church up the road' to them. Churches working together makes good use of limited resources—of the fact that St Portly's has a vast, comfy hall and kitchen but few people under the age of 90, St Genevieve-the-Less has a keen group of arc-welders and knitters but no contact with children, and the Wild 'n' Free Church has great links with the school and a thriving toddler group but has to meet in a decommissioned portaloo.

One of the glories of Messy Church is that it is church at its most pared down, so issues around robing or not robing, which form of the Creed to use, or whether to sing from a particular hymn book or to a CD backing track, simply don't arise. You can just get on with what you do best: sharing your love of Jesus with families in your community and growing church around them. This allows God's Holy Spirit to shape them, you and the mysterious thing we call 'church' that happens when people come together in Jesus' name.

With prayers for a fruitful, timely and creative relationship as you work these things out together.

A MORE RECENT LETTER TO THE CHURCHES IN CLODPOOL-IN-THE-MARSH

Dear Helen, Revd Higgins and Pastor Percy

Thank you for your letter and photos from your most recent Messy Church. I particularly like the one of Revd Higgins dressed as Bathsheba, although perhaps it isn't one to show the Bishop. You must be so thrilled about the way God's working. You're right, it's not just in Clodpool, and we rejoice that people all over the world are feeling their way into the kingdom through Messy Church. However, for you it's Clodpool that matters, as that's where God has called you to minister and live and work, and you are his hands and feet there. If we get too excited about the big picture, we might forget the huge importance of the tiny part of it for which we're responsible. The signs of growth you write about matter massively, cosmically. The comment from the six-year-old over the spaghetti about death; the smile on the face of the great-grandmother as she watched the families streaming into church; the mum who told you over the bath bombs what a rough time she's having with her abusive boyfriend; the dad who spent the whole hour helping to build David's palace out of junk instead of hiding behind the newspaper as he did the first time he came—all these moments are rare and precious and significant in themselves. They are paving the way for other wonderful things to happen in the future.

Yes, Messy Church keeps on growing, although we've no idea how much longer it will grow numerically. I can only think that the continuing wave of energy and goodwill across the world is God's Spirit taking advantage of the opportunities given to him by changes in the church and in society. Bishop Graham Cray calls these changes new imagination about the church, new permission from church leaders and new resources (*e-xpressions* e-newsletter, August 2009). I'd add to that a growth in humility in the church, and a timely acceptance that we can't insist on everybody doing things 'as we think they should be done, as they have always been done', which has been a terrible cork in the bottle for reaching people in a fast-changing society. Church is no longer at the privileged centre of society in places like the UK; it's where it belongs, on the messy edge, where it can do most good and take most risks.

As for the changes in our society that give God's Spirit space to flourish (in other forms of church as well as the Messy sort), we can see the effect of developments such as the postmodern lack of trust in authority, making parents more inclined to stay with their children than to trust the church to teach them whatever it likes. There's also a sense of families being fragmented and parents feeling unskilled through not having trustworthy models to copy for parenting, or being geographically distant from the different generations of their extended family. For a growing number of people, there's the longing for somewhere to belong in a broken society—a longing for community. Financial pressures on families mean that anything offering free food and entertainment is worth considering. I wonder too if 'tasting and seeing' the schools of thought that leave us isolated on an impersonal, hopeless, godless and purposeless planet has given people who are bringing up children a desire for a kinder world view that sees love at the start and end of life. Such a world view values love as the cause, purpose, hope and sustaining force of life. This is the love shown gently in story and in action by a community of people; it comes to them when they experience the joys, wonder and brokenness of modern family life; and above all it meets them in the most wonderful person who ever lived.

Whatever the state of our society, God has wriggled through the gaps and given us this messy gift for reaching families and others for the present time. One piece of research suggests that the sheer weight of numbers of children coming to church is important, because statistically they are then more likely to become believers as adults (John Walker in 'A socio-theological critique of Fresh Expressions in the Diocese of Canterbury', January 2012, page 117, quoting R. Gill, *A Vision for Growth* (SPCK, 1994), page 39). In other words, if very few children come to church in the first few decades of the 21st century, there will be an exponentially massive drop in the number of churchgoers by 2050: people won't be 'finding their way back to church' because they will never have been to church in the first place. I can't get my head round that, but I do hope that although people of my generation tend to say, 'Church? Outdated, outclassed, irrelevant, boring,' the next generation may be saying, 'Church? Fun, food, friendly, warm, welcoming, inspiring, motivating.'

Whatever the future holds, you are part of the happy band of intrepid explorers hacking a path through the wilderness with scissors, double-sided sticky tape and glitter glue. You are helping children and adults today and tomorrow to find their way to the goodness of God and enjoy the life-changing benefits of being citizens of his kingdom. Or, if you take a more sombre attitude, we're Hansel and Gretel dropping cupcakes and sausages in the wild, witchy forest so that people can find their way safely home.

You have a few questions that have arisen since you started Messy Church. 'Helen is keen to have a Messy Eucharist, and has been hand-stitching a set of altar cloths with matching copes out of binliners and rickrack braid in liturgical colours ready for the occasion. Have you any advice?'

For what they're worth, here are my thoughts on the sacraments—those strange rites that are something meaningful in themselves and something greater than themselves, the thin places of church life where the crossover between heaven and earth can be most transparent. I think the main ones that affect Messy Church at this stage of its development are Holy Communion and Baptism, with a few Messy Confirmation services sneaking in. I haven't yet heard of a Messy Funeral, although there has been a Messy Wedding reception for a couple who met at Messy Church. Oh, the possibilities for confetti...

I think that as individual Messy Churches reach a point in their development where they feel that Holy Communion would help their congregations experience more of God's love, they should make a point of mentioning it to their Bishop, Chair of District or equivalent. Communion is one of those services that links us firmly to the rest of the church in history and geography, and we should be mindful of not being isolated in our celebration. Anglicans may feel, as we did in our Messy Church, that the prescribed liturgy, even in its most flexible form, is not appropriate. In this case, talking to your friendly authority figure is a must, to see what options are available to you (which might be more flexible than you imagine). There is a suggested Communion liturgy in *Messy Church 2*, and another way of celebrating Christ's death and resurrection in this book. However, it is important to get a balance between touching base with the wider church and letting the liturgy genuinely grow as the 'work of the people', coloured and shaped by the local context and the local people who are present. Given the existing shape of Messy Churches, where tables are central to crafts and to food, it seems logical that we might develop forms of celebrating Communion around those tables. But we need to combine respect for the mystery with a sense of fun and joy. We should have minimal verbiage, but make what there is into 'portable poetry' that sticks in the mind and goes home with the family. Also ensure that there are maximum opportunities for participation. We need to talk with our denominational leaders and try to change the climate to help new congregations meet God in this unique way.

Baptism and confirmation present similar issues for Messy Churches in some denominations, in that the prescribed services can be very wordy and there is no provision to make the language more similar to that used in everyday Messy Church. If services are supposed to link with the wider church, and if Messy Church is part of that wider church, it needs to be a two-way process. We shouldn't expect Messy

Church people to conform to churchy language on ceremonial occasions without expecting inherited church people to experience something of Messy Church language or liturgy. You do say something startling:

> One of our Messy Church families has asked to be baptised. This provoked something of a clerical feeding frenzy behind the scenes as we naturally all wanted them to be baptised at our own church. We have decided to tell them that they must choose a church to attend for a six-month period on Sundays, then be baptised there.

Hang on, hang on: is Messy Church a church or isn't it? Have they been committed members of that Messy Church? Why are you insisting on transplanting them to a different congregation to be baptised? Invite them to other congregations by all means, just as you might invite your Sunday morning people to try out a midweek communion to enrich their worship experience. But could you not at least give them the option of being baptised in the congregation in which they have come to faith? What message are you sending out about the authenticity of their experience at Messy Church if, when it comes to the crunch, it is not seen as a suitable place to celebrate such an important rite of passage?

While we're on the subject of rites of passage, wouldn't it be great to have more waymarkers to help people on their Christian journey? There is baptism and confirmation, but that's about it. Wouldn't it be brilliant to have rites of passage to mark the smaller but still significant steps of faith—the little steps of belonging, believing, behaving and blessing? What about ones that celebrate the joys and sorrows of family life: the new job, the death of a pet, the change of school? Or one that involves a gracious leaving ceremony for those who move on to another congregation or church, or go off to college, or move house: something that celebrates what God has already done and blesses the departure and next stage of life? Or what about confirming *everybody every year* in an annual party celebration, giving us *all* the chance to recommit our lives to God for the next year? The ceremony could be woven into a seasonal pattern so that it could be planned for and looked forward to, allowing people to observe it before they actually say those words for themselves. I don't have the wisdom to create these ceremonies yet, but you might.

You mention:

> We seem to be attracting more mums than dads. Indeed, when Revd Higgins put on his Bathsheba costume, he blended in perfectly. Our few dads run the risk of being ignored or flirted with. Pastor Percy had to flee the advances of one grandmother who was worryingly intent on initiating him into the art of herbal foot massage. How can we appeal to dads too and redress the balance?

Even in our egalitarian society, it's still more usual for mums to do things with children than for dads. However much we fight it, Messy Church can still look like something for children. But for the children's sake as well as for the dads' sake, we need male role models. We need the men to feel at home there and part of any journey their family is on. Here are a few strategies that may be helpful:

✣ Make sure there are men on the core team. Another Messy Church leader was bewailing the same problem. When I asked how many men they have on their team, she looked startled and said, 'Oh! None!'
✣ Drag a man on to the planning team to ensure that the range of activities includes blokey things done in a blokey way. This doesn't exclude women or girls. When Manly Pete brought his manly saws, hammers and workbench to make wooden boats in our Messy Church, of course there were just as many females as males having a go.
✣ Have activities that aren't 'making something to take home' but are just things to do, for example, science experiments, or things to construct or destroy, ideally noisily or in a smelly way. Gross is good. Big is good. Competition works well: who can achieve the

highest, biggest, fastest or longest…? And technology has its place, with judicious use of cameras to make videos, and computers to facilitate comment on what is important in the news, life or Messy Church itself.

✤ Encourage some Manly Men to look over your publicity and handouts. Have you inadvertently excluded them with your design or wording?

But all this is relatively trivial. It's the quality of friendships more than anything else that will make men and women, children and teens want to come. And by the way, it's worth having a look at organisations like the wonderful Who Let The Dads Out? (read the book, BRF, 2012), which focus on dads spending time with their children.

'Pastor Percy's neighbour, Hannibal, enjoyed coming till September, but then started at secondary school and now considers Messy Church something just for children.' There are two lines of thought on teenagers. One is that they need a church congregation that is specific and exclusive to young people. The other is that they need to be part of an all-age congregation for their own sake and for the sake of those younger than them (who need role models) and those older than them (who need their prejudices challenging and help with their iPhones). I think both are true. As far as Messy Church is concerned, the teenagers who attended a consultation day about their role in Messy Church came back to us loud and clear with the message that their Messy Church is the only place they can hang out with younger and older people, and they value that. Teenagers, however, also need a supportive peer group so that they don't end up simply childminding or endlessly discussing what they want to do when they leave school.
 · If your teenager happens to be someone who isn't interested in helping others, serving the wider community, making things, leading from the front or simply being with other people, it's no use saying what we usually do, which is, 'Get the teenagers on to the leadership team as quickly as possible.' Messy Church will appeal to some teenagers and not to others, just as a youth congregation will appeal

to some teenagers and not to others. Perhaps it appeals primarily to those young people who are looking for a ministry within the church. The key is in relationships, in knowing your young people well and looking imaginatively at what they can give to and receive from a church as they go through a time of rapid change in their lives. It's about remembering that Messy Church is only one part of a wider church, which of course means that keeping strong links with that wider church is important.

> Revd Higgins is concerned about Messy Church being 'church lite'. He feels the need to preach a sermon series on Romans over the next twelve months to give the Messy congregation some proper teaching, but we're finding it hard to come up with many crafts on the theme of justification by faith.

Our friend and mentor Revd Dr George Lings pointed out the very useful image of the triangle of learning that makes for good all-round discipleship. It involves three equally important sides of learning: formal learning (for example, from sermons), informal learning (such as that which goes on around craft tables) and social learning (what we pick up by being with other people). Messy Church gives oodles of opportunities for informal learning (chatting through Bible stories; picking up creative skills; discussing spiritual matters; singing and praying) and for social learning (watching how other families behave; seeing what a Christian community is like; sitting and eating with people). But, in its current state, there is less opportunity for formal learning. A traditional church service, on the other hand, gives plenty of opportunity for formal learning (through sermons and Bible studies) but less opportunity for informal or social learning, except over coffee afterwards, and of course at home groups during the week. So we need to value the different types of learning already going on at Messy Church and not assume that formal learning is the only valid approach to discipleship.

In one piece of research, Messy Church is likened to the shallow end of a swimming pool, a safe place for families to play and grow in confidence as they learn to swim, dive and break out into deeper water. However, the deep end isn't empirically 'better' than the shallow end: you can't do handstands underwater at the deep end; you can't relax there with a toddler; Peter couldn't have run to Jesus through the depths of the Sea of Galilee. It's simply different, and there are things you can do there that are impossible at the shallow end.

Church is about helping each other to grow towards God, whatever stage we or they are at, not abandoning what is good just because other people look down on it. What was Paul really saying when he wrote, 'When I became a man, I put the ways of childhood behind me' (1 Corinthians 13:11)? Was he really applauding himself for leaving behind the ways of childhood or was he regretting their loss? Jesus certainly saw children as models of discipleship (Matthew 18:2–4) rather than seeing childhood as a state to be abandoned as quickly as possible. It may be topsy-turvy, but we should expect that. It's part of God choosing the 'foolish' things of the world to shame the 'wise' (1 Corinthians 1:26–28).

The place for formal learning for a Messy congregation may be outside the actual Messy Church in a much smaller group, so that it doesn't try to take everyone on a journey that might be too fast, too soon for some. Some Messy Churches are experimenting with groups and courses. Perhaps you should look imaginatively at the range of programmes available and find one that will appeal to the people in your care, rather than imposing something alien and potentially off-putting on the actual Messy Church gathering. But do value the discipling that is happening at your Messy Church—the gentle, ongoing role-modelling and mentoring that mean so much and are so easily overlooked.

You finish with a very affirming statement: 'What an impact we're having on the families who come. What lifelong memories we're helping to create. Church is about Jesus and blessings. Messy Church has changed our children's concept of church, and ours.' Many of us would echo that awe and wonder, partly because it feels so unlikely that God would choose to work in such a direct way through people like us, and partly because we're asking questions about things in church that we've always taken for granted: who is it for—believers or those who don't believe? What does hospitality mean—does it flow one-way or has the 'guest' as much to contribute as the 'host'? How are we best 'fed'—through being served or through serving others? What should we be aiming for in our faith development—to become more or less childlike? Is 'fun' the opposite of 'respectful'? Is the one church gathering the main or only aspect of being church? Are we better together or apart?

We don't know what the future holds for Messy Church. But we have 2000 years of wisdom to draw on, a church family from many different countries and of differing expressions and denominations, together with the best guide in history to steer us through, so there's plenty of help at hand to make sure that whatever happens as Messy Churches spread, grow, make mistakes and work miracles, Jesus is at the warm heart and the messy edge of everything.

May God be with you in the messiness of your painting, your praising and your planning.

[The final quotation attributed to the Clodpool team is adapted from an email from Elaine Trendell in South Australia in January 2012:

Our special speaker for the day brought his children and wife. His son three times that evening thanked Dad for taking him to Messy Church. The next morning he thanked him again, saying that when they are in the grave together, his soul will roll across to Dad's soul and say, 'Thanks for taking me to Messy Church, Dad.' Think he loved it. What an impact on a child, and that's only one. What a lifelong memory. Church is about Jesus and blessings. Messy Church has changed our children's concept of church, and ours.]

A LETTER TO THE CHURCHES IN
CLODPOOL-IN-THE-MARSH SOME TIME LATER

Dear Helen, Revd Higgins and Pastor Percy,

So you've celebrated your fifth Messy birthday! Congratulations! The cake sounds amazing. It was very brave of you to use five fireworks instead of candles, and I'm so glad the subsequent 'pebble-dashing' effect of the cake decorations on the hall walls came off with white spirit and a chisel. You probably don't realise what you and your team have achieved in establishing your Messy Church and running it for five years. It really is a major achievement to have got it off the ground jointly, making the most of the differences between your three churches. That you've maintained it all this time so faithfully, when it's such hard work and requires so much creativity, imagination and sheer sweat to make it happen, is amazing. You say you're getting up-and-down numbers, but average out at about 50–60 people each time. Just think how many families you've touched with God's love over the last five years. Phenomenal.

Despite this celebration, you wrote because you are all feeling a bit down, having received discouraging feedback from two sources, the first being someone within your own church.

> St Genevieve's has a new curate fresh from theological college who is far more up to date than we are with the latest cutting-edge thinking on mission and discipleship. She's proposed shutting down the Messy Church for the following reasons: nobody has become a Christian in the five years we've been running, and nobody wanted to go on an Alpha Course from it. Also, she has critically analysed the last three sessions and found that we are too heavy on 'blessing' and not 'challenging' enough. All in all, she can't see the justification for continuing.

It's always useful to have an outside eye to look afresh at what we do and to offer critical reflection. At the same time, we need to be confident in what we're doing when we trust it's where God has led us, and where we can see him at work, even if that isn't in the way we'd expected. As an aside, it's worth noting that the provision for training on all-age or children's ministry in many theological colleges in the UK is minimal, and it would be interesting to ask how long your curate has spent studying either of these disciplines. I suspect you may have more hands-on experience and knowledge than she does, even if you don't have the academic language to frame it— although her wider reading on mission and discipleship will no doubt prove very helpful.

Your Messy Church isn't a course for people to pass or fail. It's a church that welcomes people in, whatever their belief or way of life, and invites them to encounter Jesus. We may have made that once-for-all commitment to follow Christ—when we deliberately opted into the process of becoming more like him—and your congregation members may not have 'become Christians' in this sense. However, they may well, by God's grace and your faithfulness, be in the process of 'becoming Christians', which in a way we all are. Your Messy Church isn't like dropping in on a distant relative; it's like a parent bringing up children, there for the long haul as they come and go, fight with you, laugh with you and weep on you. No parent expects a child to grow up overnight. It's a gradual process in which the parents' role is to know when to step in and when to let go, but most of all to be there faithfully, shaping their child's life and values, which in turn shapes the person they are and the impact they have on the world. It's also about being able to let go at the right time.

Research indicates that the process of becoming a disciple can take years. Many of the people coming to Messy Church are not only miles away from any knowledge of Christianity, they may also be closed and hostile towards it, or apathetic and lacking expectancy about what it can offer (John Finney, *Finding Faith Today* (Bible Society, 1992), pages 22–25). What you're doing is helping those people to grow in knowledge and understanding about what it means to be a Christian, who Jesus is and how they can see God's fingerprints in the world and their lives. You're also opening them up emotionally to realise that church can be a happy, welcoming and fun place and one that makes them grateful for the blessing it is for them and their children. You're making church part of their family story. That's a very tall order, but you're actually doing it!

Yes, some Messy Churches have found courses like the Alpha Course, the Start Course, the Puzzling Questions Course, the Emmaus Course or the Journeys Course helpful tools to help individuals to grow in understanding and faith. They've been imaginative and discerning about who to invite on such courses and have been overjoyed to see people come to a personal faith and to baptism. But putting someone through a course isn't the only sign of growth and blessing. The rest of your letter showed many signs of the kingdom working their way through your congregation. Just look at how your team is working so happily together, even managing to resolve the knotty 'wholewheat or ordinary pasta' dispute without schism; the way your team member stood by the mum going through her messy divorce and kept her going with phone calls, emails and lattes; the way the double rainbow appeared over St Portly's at the very moment you came to that point in the story of Noah; the way the whole of Year 4 at Clodpool Primary School is buzzing about faith since eight-year-old Blair introduced them to the Yo-Yo of Doctrine that he made at Messy Church.

What about the signs that God is finding his way into family life? There's the mum who was corrected by her child for saying 'Jesus Christ!' ('Jesus wouldn't like that, Mummy.') There's the bath-time singing of Messy Church songs. There's the Messy Grace being said at mealtimes. There's even the way one family has started championing the local foodbank since you made it an issue last year. And as for the change in Horace Ramsbotham the treasurer—well!

Horace has had a change of heart, and since seeing his own grandchildren becoming regular Messy members after he'd given up all hope of them ever coming to church, he is trying to force us to spend more, rants at every church meeting about the need to fund mission and discipleship realistically, has signed up for the

Mission-Shaped Ministry Course and has increased his personal giving by 30 per cent.

Even if Mrs Penworthy-Smythe continues to stand outside your Messy Church every month with a placard saying, 'Take the mess out of church,' you say the families quite enjoy seeing her there and that several have presented her with Christmas chocolates as if she is a sort of lollipop lady. There seems to have been a whole lot of growth in godly things in your community, in personal relationships, in faith at home, in service and in individuals since you started your Messy Church. Very mustard-seedish. Very yeasty.

As for the emphasis you put on 'blessing' rather than 'challenge' in the themes you choose—what can I say? I can't imagine you're lying to people about the cost of being a disciple of Christ, telling them it's all sunshine and roses. But what do people need to hear first and loudest? How much God wants to change them or how much he loves them unconditionally, just as they are? Maybe something we've inherited from past generations of church has been a voice that says, 'No! You've got to stop! You're not good enough!' louder than it says, 'God loves you even more than you love your nearest and dearest—he loves you just for being you. You can never do anything that will cut you off from his love. God's plan for you is one of hope, adventure, purpose, safe boundaries and happy endings.' We may be loading the scales too much on one side, but that's partly to counterbalance the weight of the inheritance we're dealing with. A helpful piece of advice current among Bible storytellers is not to give children things to unlearn, however imaginatively you work with the story. You could apply the same principle to doctrine.

The other discouragement you told me about was from the area's 'What's happening in the churches?' roadshow:

We put up a display of photos from Messy Church, had a tray of cupcakes, and set up several crafts for people to try. But when the Archdeacon arrived at our display he told us we should change our

Messy Church to a Sunday, hold it every week and make sure that people started coming to Sunday church out of it.

The problem here isn't what you're doing, or how or when you're doing it—it's a misunderstanding on the part of the Archdeacon as to what Messy Church is all about. It wouldn't hurt to drop him a non-confrontational line and explain why you're doing things the way you're doing them. BRF has produced a leaflet for ministers explaining what Messy Church is, which we can send to you if it would help; a DVD that shows Messy Churches in action; and a range of published resources. We provide as much information as we can on the website; we continue to be available for training events in circuits, dioceses or individual churches; and we will happily go and chat to any denominational leaders or groups who would like a one-to-one conversation about it.

Helen is wondering about leaving the core team as she feels exhausted and has run out of cereal boxes. Pastor Percy is moving on to a post in Guatemala at the end of the year and Revd Higgins has been given another six parishes to look after. We are not sure what the future holds for Messy Church here in Clodpool.

When are we ever sure what the future holds? We try to be faithful and wise in the present, but the future isn't our responsibility. God has always used 'people moving on' to advance the spread of the kingdom: look at the way the early disciples of Jesus fled persecution in Jerusalem and spread the gospel around the Mediterranean. I know you've been giving young Britney more responsibility—have you invited her on to the core team yet? And what are you doing about giving those teenagers a real role to play in Messy Church? They sound as if they would be more than competent at some form of leadership. Perhaps you could share the load and give new people a chance to grow their own ministries by letting go of some of the responsibility.

Now you're well established and know what you're doing, it's also worth thinking about ways of re-energising your team members. Holding a monthly team meeting with treats to eat and a theme or aspect of the Messy work to consider could be very rewarding and would provide a chance for everyone to gain a better understanding of the bigger picture of what you're trying to do. You might find the extra sessions on the Messy Church DVD a good resource for themes and training. The *Get Messy!* magazine will also have a few 'focusing questions' for the team to talk about each month. In addition, BRF can organise Messy weekends in different locations, where leaders can spend time with each other and with members of the BRF Messy team, swap ideas and have a chance to take time out with God. It's the Messy equivalent of Continuing Ministerial Education. These weekends have proved popular and might be just the fillip Helen needs to help her continue her valuable ministry. It sounds as if Horace would find the funds for her to go! Discipleship is about the team just as much as it is about members of the congregation, and we must treasure each other. And we look forward to the first Messy Church in Guatemala before long.

Where will it all go from here? BRF will continue to provide a central service to Messy Churches, responding to requests for resources, ideas and advice and acting as a melting pot for the wisdom and experience that is coming in from all over the world as people make new discoveries through their Messy Churches. We'll make the most of new technologies to have a two-way relationship with Messy Church leaders. We'll continue to be advocates for ministry among families and to encourage the wider church to take it seriously. We'll do our best to support the new Messy growth overseas and to learn from those churches in their very different contexts. We'll hold the whole movement lightly and make every attempt to be partners in the gospel rather than stifling the Spirit. And, like good parents, we will try to discern when to hold on and when to let go.

You are doing such a brilliant work where it matters and with the people who matter. You're waterskiing in the wake of God's boat.

Yes, your arms ache, it's bumpy, and it hurts when you fall down, but he'll always stop and let you find your feet again—and isn't it glorious when you're on the move with him at the wheel?

With every blessing for your ongoing adventure.

Session material

Session 1

A new start

HOW DOES THIS SESSION HELP PEOPLE GROW IN CHRIST?

Forgiveness is a key part of God's rescue plan: Jesus died on the cross so that we can be forgiven. In families one of the hardest, yet most healing, things to do is to forgive each other and ask for forgiveness. This may be the start of the year, a time for making resolutions, when people are thinking about making a fresh start in all kinds of areas of life. Helping families find strategies to forgive each other could have a massive impact on the lives of children and adults.

Main Bible story: Luke 5:17–26

ACTIVITIES
---

1 Soap making

You will need: a soap kit (available from craft shops and hired out by many Regional Coordinators—check the Messy Church website for your Regional Coordinator's contact details) or bars of cheap, soft soap; table knives

Make, or carve, soap.

Talk about

Forgiveness is like washing dirt away with soap. It is like wiping away the bad things from the past and starting out all new and clean. Jesus helps us do this incredibly hard thing.

2 Gift box

You will need: small boxes or an origami pattern to make a gift box; decorative scraps; air-drying clay; sequins; beads; tissue paper; PVA glue; spreaders; pens

Make a small clay heart and decorate it with sequins and beads. Decorate your origami or ready-made box with scraps, leaving one side clear. Pad the inside with tissue paper and put the heart in. Write on the box's undecorated side, 'Forgive as the Lord forgave you' (Colossians 3:13). You can give it away as a sign that you forgive someone, or keep it to remind you to forgive other people.

Talk about
Is it easier to forgive someone or to ask for forgiveness?

3 Chalkboard scribbles

You will need: a chalkboard or pieces of board painted with blackboard paint and allowed to dry; chalk; cloths

Have fun scribbling on the chalkboard. Older people might enjoy the challenge of writing as many words as possible to do with forgiveness. Then clean the board.

Talk about
Jesus knew it was really important for people to be healed from the inside out, and he offered them forgiveness as part of their healing.

4 The big scribble

You will need: soft pencils; erasers; paper

Use the soft pencil to scribble all over the paper or to cover it with words about hurt, pain and sin, so that there are no gaps or areas of white paper showing. Use the eraser to write 'I forgive you' through the scribbling.

Talk about

Jesus saw beyond what was on the surface and spoke to people about what really mattered. For the man in the story, this was his need for forgiveness.

5 Shredding

You will need: a paper shredder; pieces of paper with pictures of people doing wrong things or descriptions of sins and shortcomings on them

Invite people to find a piece of paper that means something to them or is part of their own life. Encourage them to put it through the shredder as a sign that they want God to forgive them and take that unhelpful action or habit away.

Talk about

Jesus wants people to be close to God, not caught up in habits and actions that cut them off from him, so he offers forgiveness to people who want to make a new start.

6 Clockwork races

> **You will need:** wind-up toys that move forwards; scraps of material; masking tape

Tell the story of the paralysed man who was let down through the roof and how Jesus forgave him his sins and told him to pick up his mat and walk. Say that this was a new start for the man. Stick a piece of masking tape down on the floor as a starting line and say that this is the new start line for us. (Make a finishing line too.) Encourage people to attach a piece of material to their chosen clockwork toy with masking tape. This represents the mat of the healed man. Invite people to race their clockwork toys from the starting line.

Talk about
How do you think the man felt when he was able to take part fully in life again?

7 New-start mat-weaving

> **You will need:** sticky tape; strips of paper or cloth about 30cm long, each with one of the following words or phrases on: new life, forgiveness, fresh start, clean slate, new beginnings, new hope, face the future, repent, sorry, clear conscience, no guilt, apologise, no shame, no blame, no resentment, faith, hope, love, trust, grace, mercy

Choose a handful of strips whose words say the most about forgiveness to you. Weave the strips of paper or cloth over and under each other to make a mat that connects all these aspects of forgiveness together. Stick tape around the edges if necessary to hold the strips in place.

Talk about

Jesus said, 'Forgive and you will be forgiven' (Luke 6:37). What do you think of that?

8 Model house

> **You will need:** large and small cardboard boxes; old crayons or dowling rods; lengths of string; sticky tape; rectangular pieces of card or cloth; paper; colouring pencils; scissors; PVA glue; spreaders

Put the box on its side. Cut a rectangular hole in the top, 1cm smaller in length than the crayon or dowling rod. Take a piece of card or cloth and stick two lengths of string to it, one at each end. Tie the free ends of both pieces of string to the crayon. Tape a small box either side of the hole in the top of the box. Poke the ends of the crayon into both boxes so that it is supported horizontally. When you turn the crayon, the string should gradually be wound up, bringing the mat up. Unwind the string to lower the mat. Make the scene inside the house using paper, scissors and colouring pencils. Include figures of Jesus and the people inside. Cut out paper figures of the man and his four friends. Lay the man on the mat and put the friends on the roof. Retell the story using the model.

Talk about

Which part of this story do you think is the most important?

9 Puffy-paint writing

> **You will need:** 4 dessert spoons each of flour, salt and water; 1 dessert spoon of baking powder; food colouring; a bowl; squeezy bottles or brushes or self-sealing food bags; sheets of card; a microwave (optional)

Mix up the dry ingredients and add food colouring and water to make a thick paint consistency. People could either use a brush to paint with or squirt from bottles. You could also mix up all the ingredients in a self-sealing food bag and snip off a corner to make a painting tool. Invite people to write 'forgive' or paint a heart on to a piece of card. Air-dry or heat in a microwave for 20 to 60 seconds.

Talk about
Why do you think Jesus said to the man in today's story, 'Your sins are forgiven,' when the man hadn't told him about any sins?

10 Cross of forgiveness

> **You will need:** water bombs; runny, washable paint; a wooden cross or a large picture of a cross on a sheet of cardboard; marker pens

This is one for outside. Set up the wooden cross or attach the cardboard cross to a wall or fence. Fill the water bombs with runny paint and write on them in marker pen one of the following words: pride, laziness, despair, greediness, selfishness, envy, idolatry, nastiness, gossip, meanness, cruelty, spite, horribleness, bad temperedness, tantrums, disobedience, letting friends down or cowardice. Leave some blank in a separate container. Give three to each person and explain that these are things we all struggle with at one time or another. Jesus died on the cross so that we could be forgiven from them all. We can take them to the cross and get rid of the guilt we feel because of them. Encourage people to throw their bombs at the cross as hard as they can. Now ask them to pick a blank water bomb and write on it something only they and God know they need to bring to the cross, and then throw that one too.

Talk about
You'll have done enough talking by now on this activity.

CELEBRATION

Tell the story from Luke using people to play the parts of things and characters in the story.

First we need a HOUSE—who can be the walls of the house? Now we need someone to be JESUS and some really clever people to be the PHARISEES and TEACHERS OF THE LAW. Could you all sit in the house listening to Jesus? And we need a CROWD of people—that's everyone else. Could you come and sit here around the house, trying to get as close as you can to Jesus?

> One day Jesus was teaching, and Pharisees and teachers of the law were sitting there. They had come from every village of Galilee and from Judea and Jerusalem. And the power of the Lord was with Jesus to heal the sick.

Now we need four FRIENDS and someone to be the MAN WHO COULDN'T WALK (someone small). Let's put the man on the blanket. Now can you carefully carry the blanket with him on it to the front door of the house where Jesus is?

> Some men came carrying a paralysed man on a mat and tried to take him into the house to lay him before Jesus. When they could not find a way to do this because of the crowd...

Oh dear! There's no way through to Jesus. But look at that little outside staircase that leads to the flat roof. Can you take him carefully up there? Now can you lift off the tiles? And the reeds and straw holding the ceiling together? Oooh, Pharisees and teachers—what's all that dirt coming down on your heads? And very gently, friends, lower the man down in front of— not on top of! —Jesus.

> ... they went up on the roof and lowered him on his mat through the tiles into the middle of the crowd, right in front of Jesus. When Jesus saw their faith, he said, 'Friend, your sins are forgiven.'

Now this was a very dangerous thing to say! The Pharisees and teachers of the law didn't like that at all.

The Pharisees and the teachers of the law began thinking to themselves, 'Who is this fellow who speaks blasphemy? Who can forgive sins but God alone?'

Do you think that inside thought showed on their outside faces?

Jesus knew what they were thinking and asked, 'Why are you thinking these things in your hearts? Which is easier: to say, "Your sins are forgiven," or to say, "Get up and walk"? But I want you to know that the Son of Man has authority on earth to forgive sins.' So he said to the paralysed man, 'I tell you, get up, take your mat and go home.' Immediately he stood up in front of them, took what he had been lying on and went home praising God.

Yes, praising God. What do you think he said? What do you think he did?

Everyone was amazed and gave praise to God.

Yes, they gave praise to God too! What did they say? What did they do?

They were filled with awe and said, 'We have seen remarkable things today.'

Let's say that together: 'We have seen remarkable things today!'

Jesus healed the man on the outside, but he also healed him on the inside. He forgave the man all the bad things that were dragging him down and holding him back. Imagine what wonderful places our homes and schools and workplaces would be if we all forgave people the bad things they did to us. I wonder if we can try this month to see what it's like when we forgive people around us? It won't be easy, but Jesus is brilliant at helping us if we ask him. And we can help each other by reminding each other what today's story was about.

Prayer

Just where we're sitting, let's pass round these pens and write on the palms of each other's hands a little F, one on each palm. Now let's pray just one line from the Lord's Prayer. Put one F in the air. 'Forgive us our sins.' Now lower that F and lift up the other one. 'As we forgive those who sin against us.' Let's pray that again... and again... now really quietly... now really loudly... now with our eyes shut... now opening our eyes and standing up... Just as our hands go up, our prayers go out to God from the inside out.

And now, as God's forgiven and forgiving people, let's sing...

Sunday treat

Our Father in heaven...

This week, God, please help us to know you as our Father in heaven.
Thank you for the way you love us to bits whatever we do.
Thank you that you're always there for us, holding us tight.
Thank you that you want us to be close to you.
Thank you especially that you... **(say your own ideas)**.

Take-home idea

Go for a walk in the park, town or countryside and see how many new things you can spot—new starts of any sort, such as new bulbs sprouting, new fashions, new books or games just published, new babies or new buildings. Score a point for every new start and see who spots the most. Talk about any new starts you need to make as a family—small things like saying sorry for doing something wrong or big things like starting a new term, a new job or new nursery. Reassure everyone that God is there to help.

Messy team theme

✤ The man went away praising God; all were amazed. What has God done in your life this month that has made you praise him or be amazed?

✤ Friends are crucial in this story in bringing the man to Jesus. How can we be friends like this to the families who come to Messy Church? What can we do better?

✤ Is there anything we need to ask God's forgiveness for in the way we're leading our Messy Church?

Session 2

Love rules

HOW DOES THIS SESSION
HELP PEOPLE GROW IN CHRIST?

Jesus summarised the Law in the short command, 'Love God and love your neighbour.' These are the 'safe boundaries' that are one of the elements for a growth of love. A family life characterised by love for God and love for those around us is going to have the best chance of being a wholesome and happy one. It may be the time of year when Valentine's cards are expressing messages of love between us, but whatever month it is, love is the bedrock of our faith. Martha learned how to show love for God as much as for her neighbour when Jesus came to visit.

Main Bible story: Luke 10:38–42

ACTIVITIES

1 Paint Jesus

You will need: painting materials; good-quality paper, card or canvas; pictures of Jesus from around the world (either from doing an image search on the internet or from a pack like *The Christ We Share*, CMS/USPG/Methodist Church, 2004)

Display the images of Jesus and explain that people all over the world have tried to draw Jesus to show what they think is special about him for their country or culture. Invite people to think of a story about Jesus that they think best shows how much he loves us and to draw it in their own way, perhaps in a local setting—a school, a park, a shopping centre or a home.

Talk about
What does your picture show about Jesus' love? Why did you choose this story and setting?

2 Marbled heart

You will need: marbling inks; hearts cut out of polystyrene, styrofoam or card; water; bowl or tray; wooden kebab sticks

Decide which colours you think best represent love. Allow the marbling inks of these colours to mingle on the surface of the water in the bowl or tray. Attach the wooden kebab stick by pushing it into the point of the heart, or tape the stick to the heart if using card. Dip the heart into the ink and move it gently to make sure both sides are covered, then remove it and allow it to dry.

Talk about
What might the colours represent? Traditionally blue is for heaven or things from heaven; red indicates love, blood, passion or anger; green represents new life; yellow or gold are for riches; white indicates purity or celebration; and purple represents power or being sorry. What ingredients do you think go into love?

3 Heart-shaped planting

You will need: cress seeds or flower bulbs; sand; paper towels; pens; water

Plant your bulbs in a garden in a heart shape marked out with sand on the soil. Or draw a heart shape on a damp paper towel and try to trickle cress seeds on to the shape. If it ends up a bit messy, that doesn't matter—love can be very messy!

Talk about

The way the bulbs or seeds will grow and what helps them grow; and, correspondingly, what helps love to grow. How did Jesus show he loved people around him?

4 Volcano

You will need: bicarbonate of soda; vinegar; red food colouring; small jars without lids; play dough (optional); tablespoons; teaspoons; trays; newspaper

Press the jar up to its rim into a volcano-shaped mound of play dough on a tray. (You could use papier-mâché instead of play dough if you want the project to last longer.) Put a little red food colouring into the jar with a few tablespoons of vinegar and stir them together. Drop in a heaped teaspoon of bicarbonate of soda and watch the volcano erupt. This is infinitely satisfying—and very messy: newspaper is advisable.

Talk about

Sometimes we are so angry we feel like volcanoes about to erupt. A woman called Martha was that angry with her sister in today's story. And she very wisely chose to erupt on Jesus, who knew exactly how to make the situation better.

5 Display board or big message

You will need: the sentence 'Love God and love your neighbour as you love yourself' (based on Luke 10:27) in brightly coloured letters stuck on to card or paper; oodles of cut-out hearts in various colours and sizes; PVA glue; spreaders; felt-tip pens

Make a brightly coloured display from Jesus' summary of the Law above and glue hearts all over it to make it bright and cheerful. Alternatively take a larger heart and draw or write on it something you could do to show that you love God or your neighbour.

Talk about
In our story today, two sisters had two very different ways of showing their love for Jesus. Mary sat down and listened to him while Martha tried to make an impressive meal for him. Which sister do you think got it right? Why do you think that? Who is your neighbour? How do we show people in our own home that we love them? How do we show our neighbours on the other side of the world that we love them? How do we show God that we love him?

6 Chain bracelet or key fob

You will need: coloured paper clips or WaxiDoodles™; pony beads or similar beads with large holes; key-ring loops

Make a bracelet or key fob from the paper clips by simply sliding them together into a chain. An alternative is to make links out of WaxiDoodles™ (bendy, wax-covered modelling sticks). Add beads if desired, then clip the key-ring loop into place for the key fob.

Talk about
Churches are made up of people who are linked together by their love for God and their love for each other, like these paper clips. Can you think of any other groups of people who are joined together by love?

7 Spectacles

You will need: card; cellophane in various colours; decorative bits and bobs; pipe cleaners; templates of spectacles in different sizes and shapes (including ones with heart-shaped lenses); pictures of weird spectacles from the internet or magazines; scissors; PVA glue; spreaders; pencils

Draw a pair of spectacles on to the card using a template, and then cut them out. (An adult will probably have to cut out the holes for the lenses.) Stick on cellophane lenses and decorate wildly with as much bling as you have available, using the pictures for inspiration. Encourage people to make heart-shaped ones, although some may prefer other shapes. Wear with pride.

Talk about
Spectacles make you see things differently. What difference would it make to wear 'spectacles of love' and see everybody and everything through the eyes of love?

8 Praying hearts

You will need: a bowl of water; foil confetti hearts; pictures from today's newspaper

Invite people to drop a heart on to the water and to pray for someone who needs love at the moment.

Talk about
What difference would God's love make to the places and people in the news today?

9 Ransom message in a bottle

You will need: newspapers and magazines; paper or card; bottles with lids or corks; glitter (optional); PVA glue; spreaders; scissors; pens

In the style of an old-fashioned ransom note, cut letters out of newspapers and magazines to make the sentence 'Love God and love your neighbour as you love yourself' for older people or 'I love you' for younger people. Glue them on to the paper. Alternatively, simply write the words on to some card. Put the message in the bottle, stick a sprinkle of glitter to the sides of the bottle and seal it with a lid or cork.

Talk about
Either whether it is easier to love God, other people or ourselves, *or* what Jesus meant when he said he had come to give his life 'as a ransom for many'.

10 Martha's kitchen

You will need: ingredients: flour, sugar, butter, icing sugar, syrup, oats, cornflakes, chocolate drops, mini-marshmallows, milk and similar; kitchen equipment: bun cases, rolling pin, bowls, spoons, cutters, whisks, scales, microwave and so on

Ask a leader to play the part of Martha (they could be a man or a woman). They should invite everyone into 'Martha's kitchen' to do experimental cooking, saying, 'Here are the ingredients and implements. What can you make for our very special guest Jesus who's come to tea? Can you help me? My sister should be helping me, but she's just sitting there listening to Jesus. That's not going to be much help, is it?' and so on. The aim isn't to make perfect buns but to have the chance to mess about with the ingredients, feel them in our hands, weigh them, mix them and generally get messy.

Talk about

How cross is Martha getting? How resentful is she about Mary not helping? Are other people's siblings the same? What is more important: to provide our guest with nice food or to spend time with him?

CELEBRATION

Give everyone a square of cloth or a tissue to use in the celebration.

Martha and her sister Mary loved Jesus, and they invited him and his friends round for dinner. They needed to clean the house to get ready. *Pretend to clean with your duster. Clean the person next to you! Now open your duster and place it on your lap like a serviette.* They were so excited because Jesus was the best person ever to come to dinner and he was coming to spend a whole evening with them. How wonderful! Martha and Mary started getting dinner ready. *Can you wipe the pots with your cloth?* Then Jesus arrived with his friends. He sat down and Martha went back to the pots and pans to make dinner. *Wipe your pots out again.* But Mary sat with Jesus and listened to him. *Put your cloth somewhere right out of the way; up your sleeve or under your chair.* He was such an interesting person with so many wonderful stories, and being near him was like being near to God. She loved being close to him. She knew that listening to him was changing her life. Jesus' friends were shocked as, in those days, a woman was supposed to do the cooking. *Quick! Get your cloth and rub the pots again.* She was not meant to sit with the important guests, but Mary didn't care. *Quick! Hide your cloth again!* She just sat and listened to Jesus. Martha was still busy getting the food ready. *Quick! Cloths again!* But she had to do it all on her own now! She carried on with her busyness, getting crosser and crosser and crosser. *Get busier and busier and busier!* And she was so cross with Mary and with Jesus that she stomped up to Jesus and waved her cloth at him! *Wave your cloth with Martha.*

Then she said, 'It's not fair, Jesus! I'm doing all the work and Mary's just sitting there!'

The room went silent and Jesus said gently to Martha, 'It's so kind of you to take so much trouble to make food for us all, but sometimes being still and listening is more important. So don't be cross with your sister. Just come and sit with us for a while.'

The Bible doesn't say what happened next, but I expect they all helped to get the food on the table, don't you? I bet that shocked Jesus' friends too!

So who has been the busiest today with their duster? Being busy is important. I mean, isn't it nice to come into a lovely clean church building? It's important to keep it clean and we have people who clean here every week because they love God. And God is very pleased with them. So sometimes being busy is GOOD!

We can learn about God by coming to Messy Church, by reading about him at home and through lots of things that happen to us in our lives. So learning about God is even BETTER!

We can also listen to God like Mary did, and sometimes that can mean being still and quiet. And that's BEST of all. So I'm going to ask you to do three things.

First, be busy for God and do your busy work with the person you've come with. That's GOOD.

Now can you do something different with your duster? To remind us of learning, see if you can learn to make a figure of eight by waving your duster through the air. That's BETTER.

And last of all, I want you to hide your duster away, like we acted for Mary, and sit really, really still. That's BEST. Which one was the hardest to do? It's just like that for many of us. We find listening to God, like Mary did, is the hardest thing of all. Jesus wants us to love God completely and to love other people too. So being busy for God is GOOD. *Be busy!* Learning about God is BETTER. *Make those figures of eight!* But listening to him is the very, very BEST. *Take a moment's stillness.*

Prayer

For our prayer today we're going to be very quiet, like Mary was quiet next to Jesus so that she could listen to him. Quietly in your own heart, imagine yourself sitting next to Jesus. I wonder what he looks like. I wonder what his voice sounds like. I wonder what he says to you.

And when you're ready, come as quietly as you can to the front here and put your duster in front of Jesus' cross, as a way of saying you want to listen to him, not just here in church but at home, at school or college or work as well. Then tiptoe back to your place. We'll put some quiet music on to help.

Sunday treat

Hallowed be your name…

God, you are very holy and good and pure.
There is nothing bad in you at all.
You're like a car that runs perfectly, like the snow before anyone walks on it.
You're like… (say your own ideas).
Thank you that you are full of power but still full of goodness.

Take-home idea

Take six small pieces of white card. Leave one white and colour the rest in the following colours on one side: yellow, red, green, blue, brown. Mix them up and put them face down on a flat surface. Turn one of the pieces over and, depending on the colour, pray for the following:

✤ *Yellow:* think about those who may be ill or in pain today.
✤ *Red:* think of those who may be angry for some reason today.
✤ *Green:* think of those who are jealous and envious of others today.
✤ *Blue:* think of those who for different reasons are sad today.
✤ *White:* think of those who are frightened or afraid of something they can't easily share.
✤ *Brown:* think of those who are fed up and bored today and who might need cheering up.

Messy team theme

✤ What are the jobs you've had to do to get your bit of Messy Church ready this month?
✤ Martha was too busy to enjoy being with Jesus. How can we do everything that needs doing for Messy Church but still make time to be with Jesus?
✤ How can we help our families to enjoy just being close to him at Messy Church?

Session 3

Mothers and others

HOW DOES THIS SESSION HELP PEOPLE GROW IN CHRIST?

The timing of this session could coincide with Mothering Sunday/ Mother's Day. It's a celebration of those in our own families and in our wider community who bring us up or nurture us. This includes the church we belong to, which feeds us with food and with the stories of our faith, and gives us opportunities to enjoy life to the full. In the words of *The 8 Secrets of Happiness*, it's a chance to 'thank a mentor' and to 'invest in friends and family'. A look at the life of Jesus' own mother shows God at work in an ordinary person and demonstrates the value that he places on the role of mothers, whether that role is biological or social.

Main Bible story: the story of Mary, mother of Jesus (for Bible references see the Celebration on page 64)

ACTIVITIES

1 Spray acrylics

You will need: acrylic inks (*not* acrylic paints) in various colours; clean plant-spray bottles filled with water; different sorts and sizes of paper; masking tape

Apply drops of different coloured inks to one edge of the paper. Spray them with water from the spray bottle and tilt the paper, if you want to. Watch the colours blend with each other.

Older people could arrange masking tape in the shapes of flowers on the paper before adding the ink and water, and then let the colours flow around them. When the tape is peeled off after the ink has dried, paper-coloured flower shapes should remain.

Talk about

Just as this paper is now covered in different colours, so the Church welcomes in all sorts of different people. If you feel you're different from other people, that's great! The church wouldn't be the same without you. We are each unique, but more beautiful when we're together.

2 Secret messages

You will need: white candles or wax crayons; watery dark paint; brushes; white paper

Invite a younger person to use the crayon or candle to draw or write a message for a mother or grandmother at Messy Church, pressing down firmly as they go. The person they've written to can reveal the message by painting the dark, watered-down paint over the top of it.

Talk about

It's fun to share something special with someone who loves us.

3 Family spinner

You will need: card circles about 15cm in diameter; cocktail sticks; felt-tip pens; scissors

Choose a family you know to pray for. Using a pen, divide the card circle up into segments—one for each person in that family. Write the name of a family member in each segment and/or draw a picture of them in it with felt-tip pens. Decorate the spaces between the people with patterns. Stick the cocktail stick through the middle and use it to spin the circle. It will come to rest on one segment; pray for the person who corresponds to that segment.

Talk about
In the church family we all look after each other. One way we can do this is to pray for each other.

4 Chocolate people

You will need: melted Fairtrade chocolate—milk, white and dark—in bowls; greaseproof paper; teaspoons; pencils; scissors

Draw small and large figures on the greaseproof paper and fill in the outline with melted chocolate dribbled on with a teaspoon. Make several in different colours and allow the chocolate to set. Peel off the paper and eat. Alternatively, cut out a person shape from greaseproof paper and use it as a template to dribble chocolate over, then peel the paper off while it's still a little runny.

Talk about
In the church, we might all be different ages, sizes, colours and shapes, but we look after each other.

5 Nappy slime

You will need: clean disposable nappies; water; measuring jugs; zip-lock bags; bowls; food colouring; stirrers; scissors; bucket; spoons

Prepare this at home, wearing a mask to avoid inhaling the dust. Cut the absorbent padding out of the nappy, discard the rest of the nappy, shred up the padding and divide it between about four zip-lock bags.

At Messy Church, stir a few drops of food colouring into some water in a bowl. Then encourage people to have fun seeing how much coloured water they can add to their bag of nappy shreds without it turning to mush. It's quite amazing just how absorbent the nappy shreds are. Have fun squashing the bag. This is not one to be taken home, and fairly obviously, don't eat it.

Talk about
Mums and carers have to do a lot of things to look after children, including dealing with not-so-clean nappies. When did you last say thank you to the person who looks after you for doing things they would rather not do?

6 Coffee-cup cosy

You will need: old socks; sewing gear; mug to show size required; decorations: felt shapes, beads and so on; PVA glue

Cut the sock above the heel and discard the 'foot' part. Cut a hole in the remainder for the mug's handle. It is unlikely to need hemming around the bottom edge. Add decorations if required to make a coffee-cup cosy as a present for a coffee or tea-drinking parent or carer. If you can source cheap mugs, you could include one with the cosy.

Talk about
What do you love about the person who brings you to Messy Church?

7 Window card

You will need: old window envelopes; card; scraps of collage paper; felt-tip pens; scissors; PVA glue; spreaders; sticky tape

Cut the window out of the envelope. Fold a piece of card down the middle so that it stands up. Cut a rectangle out of the front side that is 1cm smaller than the window in both width and length. Glue or tape the window behind the hole. Draw a picture (perhaps of a flower) on the inside so that it shows through the window when the card is shut. Decorate the rest of the front of the card with collage pieces to make it look like a house with a window.

Talk about
What do you like best about the person who looks after you at home?

8 Icing flowers

You will need: home-made or ready-to-roll icing in seven different pale colours; dental floss; rolling pin; icing sugar for rolling; icing sugar mixed with water to make a sticky paste; buns or biscuits

Make seven rods about 0.5cm in diameter and 10cm long out of each colour of icing. Surround one rod with the other six and gently press them together so that they stick. Use the dental floss like a cheese wire to slice off flower shapes along the length of the log. Spread the icing sugar paste on to the bun or biscuit, and then decorate with the icing flowers.

Talk about

Giving someone flowers is another way of saying, 'I love you.' It's a good idea to tell people we love them, even if we think they know already. In fact it's a good idea to tell them every single day!

9 Flower brooch

> **You will need:** old silk scarves or other very thin and flimsy fabrics; safety pins; thread or wool; scissors; sticky tape

Cut a rectangle of cloth about 15cm x 6cm. Roll it into a loose cylinder 6cm high and seal one end with tape. Bind it tightly with wool or thread about halfway up. Cut slits down from the unsealed end (as if you're making palm branches out of a roll of paper) and gently move the different layers of fabric upwards to cascade over each other like petals. Put a safety pin through the back of the flower and wear it as a brooch.

Talk about

Jesus said that anyone who does what God wants them to is his mother or brother or sister (Mark 3:35). What do you think he meant?

10 Newspaper apron

> **You will need:** broadsheet newspapers; wool; sticky tape; a hole punch; paint; copies of the Messy Church splat; PVA glue; spreaders; scissors

Lay two or three sheets of newspaper on top of each other, and fold them in half lengthways. Cut a shoulder-shaped arc out of the open side of the paper through all the thicknesses so that when you open it up it looks apron shaped. Fold the top edge down 3cm. Tuck a length of wool under the fold and tape the fold down. Tie the ends of the wool so that it sits comfortably around your neck (taking care that it doesn't get tangled around children's necks). Punch holes in the sides and attach a length of wool through each hole to let you tie it behind you. Cover with paint handprints or stick on the Messy splat.

Talk about
Real love is about putting someone else first. Jesus showed his love for us by going to the cross for us. We could show our love for other people by helping them—and that might mean getting messy.

CELEBRATION

For each part of the story you could either use a copy of a Giotto painting or an object as suggested below.

This is the story of a young woman who decided to say 'yes'. 'Yes' is only a small word, but sometimes a 'yes' can change everything. I wonder what you will think of the 'yeses' in our story today?

Picture 1 (The Annunciation) or a figure of an angel, Luke 1:26–38

Mary was only a teenager when she saw an angel in her home. The angel told her she was going to have a baby called Jesus. Although she was scared, Mary believed the angel. She said, 'Yes. I want this to happen just as you have said.' This was the first 'yes' that Mary said to God.

Picture 2 (The Visitation) or a magnifying glass, Luke 1:39–56

But this 'yes' wasn't easy. What were people going to say? Mary travelled to visit her cousin Elizabeth near Jerusalem. She too was having a baby and when they met, Elizabeth's baby jumped for joy inside her. Mary was so happy that she sang a song that magnified her joy. This was the second time Mary said 'yes'. This time she sang her 'yes' to God.

Picture 3 (The Nativity) or a model of a manger, Luke 2:1–20

Mary and Joseph travelled to Bethlehem. Mary gave birth to a baby boy and she laid him in a manger or feeding box. That night angels sang in the fields and shepherds ran through the streets, and Mary knew that her 'yes' to God was not only a surprise for her, but also for the whole world. Mary wondered about it all and kept all these things in her heart.

Picture 4 (The Presentation) or a toy sword, Luke 2:22–35

While Jesus was still tiny, Mary and Joseph travelled to the Temple to thank God for their new son. There they met an old man called Simeon who took the baby in his arms and began to praise God. And then Simeon turned to Mary and said that because of Jesus, one day Mary would feel great pain and sadness, like a sword cutting into her heart. What was he saying? What was her 'yes' going to mean?

Picture 5 (Jesus Lost at Twelve Years Old) or a scroll, Luke 2:41–52

When Jesus was twelve years old, Mary and Joseph travelled to Jerusalem again. But on the way home they noticed Jesus wasn't with them, so they went back to look for him. They found him in the Temple and Jesus said, 'Didn't you know I would be in my Father's house?' Mary and Joseph didn't understand. Joseph's house was in Nazareth. But Mary accepted what Jesus said. She said 'yes' to his strange words. This was the third time she had said 'yes', as she began to realise that her child was not her own son to keep.

Picture 6 (At the Cross) or a cross, John 19:25–27 with references to Luke 8.19–21 and John 2.1–10

When Jesus was a man, he left his home in Nazareth and set out to tell everyone about the kingdom of God. Mary let go of her child. She had to say 'yes' again. Mary simply told people, 'Just do whatever he tells you.' She encouraged them to say 'yes' to Jesus.

Perhaps Jesus had learned from Mary how to say 'yes' to God. Because Jesus said 'yes' to God, he went to the cross to put things right. Beneath that cross, Mary stood weeping, because she knew that her 'yes' was part of all this pain. It was like a sword cutting into her heart. And Mary held her son in her arms once again and said 'yes' to God.

Picture 7 (The Ascension and/or Pentecost) or a model of a dove, Acts 1:14

God said 'yes' to Jesus. God brought him back from the dead. Mary saw that great day. Mary was there when the Holy Spirit came so that thousands more people could say 'yes' to God too.

This is the story of a woman who decided to say 'yes'. 'Yes' isn't an easy word, but it is a word that can change the world. Mary said 'yes' to God and Jesus said 'yes' to God, so that God will say 'yes' to us. And now we can say 'yes' to others in the name of Jesus. Perhaps your 'yes' will be one that changes the world too.

✣ I wonder which part of this story you like best?
✣ I wonder which 'yes' was most important?
✣ I wonder what 'yes' you want to say to God?

Prayer

Use a large version of the family spinner from craft activity 3 (page 59), with 'Mum', 'Dad', 'Grandma', 'Grandpa', 'brother', 'sister', 'pet' and so on written on, rather than particular names. Spin this and invite everyone to call out the names of people that fit the category selected to pray for.

Sunday treat

Your kingdom come...

Our Father in heaven, your way is always the best way.

Help us to listen to you and to do what we can to make your kingdom come alive here on earth.
Especially we pray for places and people that need you, like... **(say your own ideas)**.

Take-home idea

Pick a flower and play a version of 'she loves me; she loves me not', pulling off the petals one by one—but change the words to 'God loves me; he loves me even more; he loves me loads; he loves me hugely; he loves me massively...', taking it in turns to pull off a petal and find the next way of saying how much God loves us.

Messy team theme

✢ What have you said 'yes' to this month? What difference has your 'yes' made?
✢ Mary the mother of Jesus said 'yes' to God. What difference did her 'yes' make?
✢ Are there things in your team you need to say 'yes' to? Is there anything you should say 'no' to?

Easter

HOW DOES THIS SESSION HELP PEOPLE GROW IN CHRIST?

Celebrating the seasons of the church year gives us a chance to rehearse the key stories of our faith regularly and lets them become embedded in the fabric of our lives. At Easter we celebrate the death and resurrection of Jesus. The Easter story shows us our significance in God's eyes; it demonstrates his forgiveness, provides hope of resurrection in the direst of situations and celebrates the new life of the kingdom—and it is the very reason our church exists. It reminds us that we are part of a bigger picture, a cosmic story of redemption.

Main Bible story: John 18—20

You will find a great range of special Messy Church Easter crafts from Infinite Crafts to add even more variety to what you are offering: www.inf.co.uk/infinite/Messy_Church_Craft_Kits.html.

ACTIVITIES

1 Jesus' lifeline

You will need: plain A4 paper; writing pens; felt-tip pens

Fold the paper in half lengthways. Now fold it widthways, then widthways again so that you have a 'booklet' with six sides. Make an illustrated booklet of the story of Jesus' life, assigning the pages as follows: 1: cover; 2: Jesus is born; 3: Jesus grows up and shows what God's kingdom is about; 4: Jesus dies on a cross on Good Friday; 5: Jesus comes back to life on Easter Day; 6: Jesus is always with us through his Holy Spirit and will return one day. You might want to do the writing for the younger people and let them decide how to illustrate it.

Talk about
The same Jesus who was born in Bethlehem grew up and died on a cross and came back to life.

2 Bead cross

You will need: Hama beads in various colours; pegboards; an iron and an ironing board; greaseproof paper

On the pegboard, make a small cross out of Hama beads. Choose colours that say something about what Good Friday and Easter mean to you. Put the greaseproof paper on top and let someone responsible iron it to fuse the beads into shape.

Talk about
How much of the Easter story do you know? What happened to Jesus in the last week of his life? Which part do you think is saddest? Which part is the happiest?

3 Splatter-paint a messy world

You will need: means of splatter painting—depending on size of paper and space, this could be toothbrushes, scrubbing brushes, new toilet brushes, foam balls or anything else you can flick or throw; paint; large sheets of paper; a large cross shape; pencils; PVA glue; spreaders

Draw the planet Earth on the paper and invite people to show what a mess our world is in by covering it with splatters of paint by whatever means you choose. Take the cross and glue it over the messy world.

Talk about

It may seem a strange way to put the world right, but Jesus chose to die on the cross to put us right with God person by person, family by family.

4 Coin picture

You will need: various coins; metallic silver wax crayons; different-coloured sheets of sugar paper; card; scissors; PVA glue; spreaders; pens

Put a coin under the paper and gently press it with a thumb until you can see its outline. Rub over it with a crayon to bring out the pattern. Make several rubbings. Cut them out and stick them on to a piece of card in an interesting design. Write across the top how much you think you are worth.

Talk about

The chief priests paid Judas Iscariot 30 pieces of silver to betray Jesus to them. How do you think Jesus felt when one of his best friends 'grassed him up' like this? How do you think Judas felt when he realised what he had done? Have you ever been let down by a friend? Have you ever let a friend down?

5 Passion-week display

> **You will need:** pictures to colour showing Palm Sunday, Jesus overturning the tables in the temple, the Last Supper, Jesus being arrested, the crucifixion, Jesus' burial and Easter Day; paint or collage materials to colour them in; brushes; PVA glue; spreaders

Fill the pictures with colour and tell each other the story of what happened to Jesus in the last week of his life.

Talk about
How does the story fit together? Can you tell it all from Palm Sunday to Easter Sunday using the pictures? And can you remember what happens next?

6 Egg painting

> **You will need:** wooden or hardboiled eggs; paints; fine-tipped brushes; felt-tip pens

Traditional designs for *pysanky,* or Eastern European painted eggs, include the following: a triangle representing the Holy Trinity; tripods representing birth, life and death; spirals representing the mystery of life and death; dots representing Mary's tears; and hearts representing love. Decorate your egg with paint or pens to include one or more of these symbols. Have an egg-rolling race.

Talk about

Symbols are ways of saying things without words, and they can have hidden meanings. What hidden meanings does Easter have, do you think?

7 'New life' table decoration

> **You will need:** oasis foam; table knives; wooden kebab skewers; dish; wire or sticky tape; flowers and greenery

Make a small cross out of the foam using the table knife and, if necessary, pin it together with two skewers (get an adult to do this first step). Anchor it in the dish with wire or tape. Cover it with fresh flowers and fill in the gaps with greenery. Use it as a table centrepiece.

Talk about

Jesus' cross was a place of death, but also the place new life came from, just like these flowers coming out of the oasis cross.

8 Two-sided cross

> **You will need:** wooden or cardboard crosses; dark and bright paint; brushes; PVA glue; spreaders; glitter or sequins; thread; sticky tape; stiff card

Paint one side of the cross in colours of sadness and pain; then paint the other side of the cross in colours of joy and new life. Add glittery things to this side if you want to make it even more vibrant. Stick on a thread to hang it up by, or glue it to a base of stiff card so that it stands up and both sides can be seen.

Talk about
Can you have the joy of Easter without the pain of Good Friday? Can you have the pain of Good Friday without the joy of Easter?

9 Easter eggcitement buns

> **You will need:** plain buns; green fondant icing; small chocolate eggs (Fairtrade if possible); cake sparklers

Encourage people to make an Easter scene on the bun by moulding a tomb out of the green fondant icing and using an egg as the stone that was rolled across the entrance. Keep the buns for teatime, but before you bring them out, stick a cake sparkler in the tomb. Everyone could light their sparklers at once to show the power, excitement and unexpectedness of that first Easter Day.

Talk about
The women discovered Jesus was alive again—that was an even bigger surprise for them than the sparklers were for us!

10 Woodwork

> **You will need:** small blocks of wood; sandpaper; hammers; nails

This is one for older people. Sand down the wood to remove any splinters. Nail two pieces of wood together to make a cross. Add more nails if you want to.

Talk about
Jesus was a carpenter. Mary would have been used to hearing the sound of nails being hammered into wood by Joseph and by Jesus.

CELEBRATION

Entrance song: 'He came down that we may have love' (Cameroon traditional).

Invite the whole congregation to act out the story of Good Friday together as follows:

Imagine it's night-time.

One side of the congregation: 'We're with Jesus in a peaceful garden. It's an olive grove. Jesus is praying, and we are snoozing.' *Encourage snores.* 'But we've all woken up: we can hear a crowd of angry people and soldiers coming. Oh no, they're carrying swords, clubs, lanterns and torches…'

The other side is the crowd. Choose what you're carrying and show how angry you are. It's Jesus' enemies come to arrest him!

Jesus' friends spring up. They are very afraid. They're also shocked and angry because leading the crowd is Judas. Judas used to be their friend and Jesus' friend. Now he's chosen to be their enemy. The angry mob shakes swords and clubs threateningly. Jesus' friends put up their fists ready for a fight. It looks as if there's going to be a riot… *Wave swords, clubs and so on.*

Peter draws his sword and runs forward to defend Jesus. His sword goes swish and—ow! He cuts off the right ear of a man called Malchus. Jesus steps forward and says, 'Peter, put your sword away. No more of this.' In the torchlight, all eyes are on Jesus now as he gently puts his hand on Malchus' bleeding ear. Then he takes his hand away—and Malchus' ear is completely healed.

Then Jesus allows the soldiers to lead him away as a prisoner. Both sides are still enemies to each other.

What will happen the next day? The soldiers kill Jesus on a cross. Jesus' arms are stretched wide. *Ask someone to stand in the gap between* the two sides of the congregation and reach out to both sides. Jesus stretched out his arms and died on the cross to draw enemies back together as friends; to heal all the wounds caused by anger, violence and hatred; and to make us a new family with God as our heavenly father. We're no longer divided. When Jesus died on Good Friday and came back to life on Easter Day, he gave us his peace—to share. *Invite those next to the gap to stretch across it and hold hands across the divide.* Let's thank Jesus for being a peacemaker.

Prayer

Thank you, Lord Jesus, that you stretched out your arms and died on the cross to bring us back together in peace. Help us to stretch out our hands to share your peace with everyone. Amen.

Now let's peacefully give high fives to five brothers and sisters on the side that used to be your enemy!

Sunday treat

Your will be done, on earth as it is in heaven…

Jesus, our friend, we want our bit of earth to be like heaven.
We want there to be no more death or sorrow or crying or pain.
We ask you to make our world more like heaven, with lots of… **(say your own ideas)**.

Take-home idea

Jesus was placed in a sealed tomb, but two days later he had disappeared. The following fun idea can help to explain this.

You will need: bread dough; marshmallows

1. Take a small piece of bread dough—enough to make a normal-sized bread roll.
2. Wrap the bread dough around a marshmallow, making sure that the marshmallow is completely surrounded.
3. Bake the roll in the oven at the same temperature and for the same time as you would a normal bread roll (around 220°C/425°F/Gas 7, for 8–10 minutes).
4. When it looks golden brown, take the roll out of the oven and check whether it is cooked through. You can do this by tapping on the bottom of the roll. If it sounds hollow, it should be cooked.
5. Now break open the roll. What can you see? The marshmallow should have dissolved during the baking, leaving you with a roll that is hollow inside—like the empty tomb. (The secret here is not to use too much bread dough, as the dough needs to be completely cooked for the marshmallow to disappear.)

Messy team theme

✛ What signs of new life have you seen around you this month?
✛ What signs of new life have you seen at Messy Church?
✛ What is dying and what is starting in your own life at the moment?

Session 5

The Holy Spirit

HOW DOES THIS SESSION HELP PEOPLE GROW IN CHRIST?

What happened at the first Pentecost is one of the key stories of the Christian faith. Pentecost is an important part of the church year, and gives us the opportunity to focus on the Holy Spirit. There are already activities on wind and fire in the Pentecost session in the first Messy Church book, so here we concentrate on the fruits of the Spirit. Thinking about the Holy Spirit reminds us of the mystery of our faith— that we can't see or touch God but we believe he is real nonetheless. It's a chance to remember and perhaps experience the 'otherness' of God.

Main Bible story: Galatians 5:22–23

You will find a great range of special Messy Church Pentecost crafts from Infinite Crafts to add even more variety to what you are offering: www.inf.co.uk/infinite/Messy_Church_Craft_Kits.html.

ACTIVITIES

1 Fruity flowers

You will need: small biscuit cutters in flower, heart and star shapes; wooden skewers or cocktail sticks; fruit (apples, pears, melon); base made from mini flowerpot and oasis (optional); labels with the fruits of the Spirit written on them; blender; knives; chopping boards; lemon juice in a bowl

Look through the labels and select a fruit of the Spirit that you would particularly like to grow in your life. What might that look like if it was in front of your eyes? Can you make it into a 'fruity flower'? Ask a responsible person to slice the fruit into pieces 0.5cm thick. Then use the biscuit cutters to cut out flower, heart and star shapes. Put these on to cocktail sticks so that they look like flowers on stalks. Attach the appropriate label to the stick. 'Plant' in the mini flowerpot filled with oasis if you want to display them. (You might want to dip the fruits in lemon juice first to stop them browning.) Blend the fruit off-cuts into smoothies.

Talk about
What's so special about the fruit of the Spirit you've chosen?

2 Fruitle Drive

You will need: a dice; a picture of a whole person labelled as follows: heart=1=love; smiley face=2=joy; body=3=peace; right leg=4=patience; left leg=4=kindness; right arm=5=goodness; left arm=5=faithfulness; right hand=6=gentleness; left hand=6=self-control; separate body parts cut out of card, each labelled as above—enough to make up six whole people

Have a speedy game of Fruitle Drive (couldn't see a way of bringing beetles into it). Throw the dice and build your body, adding the appropriate body part for the number you've thrown. The first one to complete their body with all nine parts is the winner. Take it in turns to roll and keep rolling the dice and adding on body parts until you roll a number that you can't use. Then pass the dice to the next person.

Talk about
Who do you know that is patient, kind, gentle, full of self-control and so on?

3 Apple pompoms

You will need: red or green wool; cardboard cut into ring doughnut shapes; brown pipe cleaners; gift tags; scissors

Wind wool around the outside of two doughnut-shaped circles of cardboard, and then tie tightly around the middle. Next, wind the brown pipe cleaner around the middle, so that it sticks up like the stalk of an apple. Finally, cut around the edge to make a pompom, and remove the cardboard. Choose the fruit of the Spirit you'd most like to grow in your family and write it on a tag to attach to the stalk. Given the usual time constraints at Messy Church, you might want to make the circles small and the wool as thick as you can find.

Talk about
Do you think the Holy Spirit is more like rain, fertiliser, air, soil or a fruit tree?

4 Hand painting

You will need: a face-painting kit

Invite people to have fruit painted on the backs of their hands to remind them of the fruits of the Spirit. Bananas, bunches of grapes, apples, pears and strawberries are all distinctive.

Talk about
When do you find it hardest to be patient, kind or gentle? Is this something you'd like Jesus to help you with?

5 Fruit mobile

You will need: stiff coloured paper; lettering stencil; templates of various fruits; a hole punch; thread; dowelling rods or coat hangers; scissors

Choose a fruit template and use it to cut out two identical fruit shapes. In one, cut a slot that goes from the top to the middle, and in the other, cut a slot that goes from the bottom to the middle. Then stencil on to them the names of some fruits of the Spirit. (You may not have time to make a fruit for each fruit of the Spirit.) Slot the shapes together at right angles. Punch a hole in the top and thread your fruit on to the hanger. Make more fruits as time allows.

Talk about

With your mobile you have a reminder that the Holy Spirit grows good things like these fruits in our lives. Also, when it moves in the breeze, you have a reminder that he breathes new life into us.

6 Blow-paint a fruit tree

You will need: straws; brown or grey watery paint; fruit stickers or cut-outs from magazines; PVA glue; spreaders; pens

Blow runny brown or grey paint in such a way as to make it into the shape of a tree trunk and branches. Add fruit stickers or pictures of fruit. Write the fruits of the Spirit around the edge as a border.

Talk about

Which of these fruits did Jesus show in his life?

7 Fruity me

You will need: sheets of paper (the bigger the better); fruit; paint in fruity colours in trays; pens

Draw a big body shape on the paper. If the paper is big enough you could get a friend to draw around you. Then use the fruit to fill up the shape with fruity printing: cut apples in half and print with them; write with a banana dipped in paint; roll an orange or a pineapple in paint and then over your shape; dip bunches of grapes in paint and splatter with them. If you feel uncomfortable about using food in this way, use plastic fruit. Older people might prefer to create a more stylised version by producing pristine rows of fruit prints across the body shape and layering them up.

Talk about
What would the world be like if everyone was just as full as this of love, joy, peace, patience and so on?

8 Family juggling

You will need: tissue paper; sheets of paper; display board; pens; stapler; scissors; PVA glue; spreaders

Draw a family group on a sheet of paper—not a nuclear family, but an intergenerational church family with people of all ages, abilities and disabilities, races and sizes standing together with their arms up and hands out. They will be juggling the fruits of the Spirit across and above their group. Make each fruit out of a fruit-shaped piece of paper covered with tissue paper to give different textures: screwed-up balls of it glued on if you have time/person-power; ripped-up strips in fruity colours if time is short. Leave a space to write which fruit of the Spirit it is across the centre of each one, and staple them above the family group. Fix the picture to the display board.

Talk about
God wants us to share these fruits around, both when we're together as a church and when we're in other groups outside church.

9 Layered landscape

You will need: scissors with zigzag blades; different colours and types of paper; PVA glue; spreaders; sheets of paper for the background

Ask people to imagine a landscape coloured by the fruits of the Spirit. Use the scissors to create stylised, non-naturalistic hillsides, mountain ranges and fields from the colours suggested by each fruit. For example, for some people, love might be red and self-control white. Layer up the landscape elements on the background paper and glue them into place.

Talk about
Where do you see God's Spirit at work in your landscape—at home, work or school, for example?

10 Fruit explosions

You will need: a home-made catapult or trebuchet made from wood, elastic and a flowerpot; a wall; overripe fruit that would have been thrown out anyway (ask at the supermarket)

Make sure you're not going to catapult things into a neighbour's garden/window/greenhouse. Ask someone who is good at woodwork to make a catapult or trebuchet beforehand that will fire fruit safely (see diagram, page 185). Ours was on a sturdy wooden base with two wooden frames nailed to it in the shape of upside-down 'Y's angled slightly backwards and braced. The elastic was attached to the highest points of the wood and held a plastic flowerpot with a ring by which to pull the flowerpot back and fire the fruit it contained. (Give this job to someone creative: they will be able to make you one to their own design!) Experiment with the fruit to see which creates the most spectacular splat on the wall. If the territory is not suitable for catapults, you could go up to a high place and drop fruit instead. For added artistic value, spread paper over the wall or floor first and enjoy the patterns.

Talk about
Spreading the fruit of the Spirit around can be done in quiet ways or in loud ways. Which suits you better? How might you spread love, joy, peace, patience and so on?

CELEBRATION

Set up a picture of a fruit tree and cut-outs of fruits, or, even better, a model of a tree like the one from Infinite Crafts (www.inf.co.uk) with fruit on it that can be removed.

Each time you mention the refrain 'like fruit from a tree', take some of the fruit from the tree and spread it out around the tree. If you have enough, you could pass a fruit to everyone during the final paragraph and encourage them to keep it to remind them of the story.

Expect people to be learning the list of fruits of the Spirit as you repeat them, and to join in with you—especially with the 'like fruit from a tree' refrain.

There was once a boy like no other child. He was full of love, joy and peace. He was patient, kind and good. He was faithful, gentle and self-controlled. He shared these good things with others *like fruit from a tree*.

He didn't have an easy life: people whispered about who his father was, and there wasn't much money. But his family had a lot of love to share around, and they showed him even more love, joy and peace; patience, kindness and goodness; faithfulness, gentleness and self-control. They shared these things with him *like fruit from a tree*.

He learned to read, and he read in the holy books about the best life of all. He read about love, joy and peace; about patience, kindness and goodness; about faithfulness, gentleness and self-control. They grew in him *like fruit on a tree*. And like no other person before or since, he lived that best life of all because he was not only a person, he was God as well.

When he grew up, in everything he did he showed even more love, joy and peace. He was even more patient, kind and good. He was even more faithful, gentle and self-controlled. His life was even more fruitful *like fruit on a tree*.

There came a time when he had to choose whether to live for himself or to live for other people and for God. He chose to live for other people and for God. And that meant he chose to give up everything—he even gave up his own life for them. He went to the cross and died there, *like fruit falling from a tree*.

But nothing can keep the Spirit of God dead for long. He had been so full of life that he came to life again, like seeds from a fruit growing into a whole orchard full of trees. So now his love, joy and peace; his patience, kindness and goodness; his faithfulness, gentleness and self-control aren't just in him. They are growing in anyone who knows him, just *like fruit on the biggest tree there has ever been*—a tree so big it has spread its branches round the whole wide world.

Prayer

Choose nine leaders or helpers to take groups into different parts of the room, each assigned with one of the fruits of the Spirit. Ask them to encourage their group to devise an action for the fruit as soon as they're together—for example, giving a hug for love or jumping for joy.

For our prayer today we're going to ask God to let his Holy Spirit grow these fruits in us. When I call out your fruit, show us your action, and on the second call, everyone repeat the action. So I will say: 'Father, Son and Spirit, help us to grow LOVE.' *The love group shows the action. Then everyone repeats,* 'Yes, LOVE!' *and everyone does the action for love.*

LEADER: *Father, Son and Spirit, help us to grow LOVE.*
ALL: *Yes, LOVE!*
LEADER: *Father, Son and Spirit, help us to grow JOY.*
ALL: *Yes, JOY!*
LEADER: *Father, Son and Spirit, help us to grow PEACE.*
ALL: *Yes, PEACE!*
(And so on.)

Sunday treat

Give us today our daily bread...

God our heavenly Father, you love to give us good things from the world you made!
Thank you especially for the food you give us, like... **(say your own ideas)**.
Thank you too for the other things we need to stay alive, like... **(say your own ideas)**.

Take-home idea

As a family, chat about what you do to celebrate a birthday.

✢ Do you buy cards or presents?
✢ Do you have a party?
✢ Do you make a birthday cake?

Ask each person what they like most about birthdays and why.

✢ Do you remember a favourite birthday, and why it was so special?
✢ What is so special about Pentecost?

You could make some party food or a birthday cake in advance and eat it at the end of your time talking together. Or you could hold a small Pentecost party for family and friends.

Messy team theme

✢ What's your favourite fruit? Why?
✢ What's your favourite fruit of the Spirit? Why?
✢ Which fruits do you see ripening in your team since you began working together?

Session 6

The Lord's Prayer

HOW DOES THIS SESSION HELP PEOPLE GROW IN CHRIST?

The theme of this session is God our Father, with particular focus on the prayer Jesus gave us to help us talk to 'our Father in heaven'. This ties in neatly with Father's Day, if it is this month. Part of the toolbox of faith, the Lord's Prayer is a valuable gift that we can pass on to the next generation. It seems sad that if children learn it at all, they often learn it in school rather than in church; even weekly churchgoing children may be out of the service when it is said. Some of the parables about prayer also feature here so that we can see exactly how Jesus is encouraging us to pray to God our Father.

Main Bible story: Matthew 6:5–14

ACTIVITIES

1 Pipe-cleaner figures

You will need: pipe cleaners; pony beads; googly eyes; funky foam; wrapped sweets or other tiny treats

Make a parent figure and a child figure out of the pipe cleaners and beads. The beads can be used as hands or feet, or threaded on to the pipe cleaners to make interesting limbs, with the funky foam added for extra interest—but let people choose how to do it, as ever. Put a wrapped treat in the hands of the parent figure and position it as if they are giving the treat to the child.

Talk about
In his famous prayer, Jesus effectively called God his 'dad', which is why we can pray to God saying 'Our Father'. Our parent figure is giving the child a gift; Jesus said God is like that loving parent.

2 Word mobile

> **You will need:** wooden coat hangers with the words 'Our Father' painted on to them (older people could do the painting during the session, but have some ready to go for younger people); ribbon or transparent thread; a hole punch; circles, hearts, squares or other interesting shapes cut from card in different colours and big enough to write a word on; pens

Challenge a family or friendship group to make a mobile with words to describe God our Father, each starting with a different letter of the alphabet. Write each word on a cardboard shape, hole-punch it and string it to the coat hanger. Further words can be added on to the coat hanger or attached by thread to the existing shapes to dangle beneath them. Here are some word suggestions to get you started, and in case you want to print some out to make it easier for people. Encourage people to use 'hallowed' for 'H'.

amazing, brilliant, childlike, daring, enterprising, forgiving, good, hallowed, invisible, joyful, kind, loving, motherly, never-failing, old, patient, quite fantastic, right, splendid, time-travelling, unavoidable, volcanic, warm, xtremely loving, young, zillions of times bigger than me

Talk about
What stories do you know about God where he displays these characteristics? Jesus said God's name is 'hallowed' or 'holy' and

told us to pray to him as a holy God. 'Hallowed be your name' is the second line of the Lord's Prayer.

3 Kingdom feelies

You will need: rising bread dough and bread dough without yeast in; seeds; small, non-toxic bulbs; tray and compost; a growing bulb or plant; pearl beads and one real pearl in a box (but only if one is available and the owner is willing to risk bringing it in!); scribble board/graffiti wall with the title 'Your kingdom come'; marker pens

Say you're taking people on a lightning tour of what God's kingdom is like. Let them poke the two sorts of dough while you tell them Jesus' parable about yeast (Luke 13:20–21). Let them plant a seed or bulb in the compost tray and then marvel at a growing plant as you tell them the parable of the mustard seed (Luke 13:18–19). Let them run the beads through their fingers and touch the real pearl in a box as you tell them the parable of the pearl of great price (Matthew 13:45–46). Now ask them to scribble on the board what they think the kingdom of heaven is like.

Talk about
This is a very talky one already, so keep it short and punchy.

4 Daily bread

You will need: white sliced bread; a variety of sauces such as ketchup, mustard, HP sauce, chocolate sauce, honey and squirty cream

Write 'daily' on the bread using any sauces you like as long as you're prepared to eat the results!

Talk about
Jesus' prayer includes the line, 'Give us today our daily bread.' Where does your food come from? Where is it from ultimately?

5 Forgive us

You will need: fire (outside or in a metal bucket, or a tea light on a fireproof surface); barbecue tongs; bucket of water

Write or draw on a piece of paper very privately something you're really sorry for and that you're determined never to do again. Write on another piece of paper something someone has done to you that has hurt you in some way and tell God you forgive them for it. Fold them both in half. Ask a responsible person to burn the two pieces of paper, using the tongs if necessary.

Talk about
This shows how completely those sins are forgiven when we give them to God, and how completely we can forgive others with God's help. The pieces of paper have completely gone and so have those sins.

6 Lolly-stick gate

You will need: lolly sticks; cardboard rectangles about 20cm x 15cm; PVA glue; spreaders; pens

Glue the lolly sticks into a five-barred gate design on the card and write around the edge as a border: 'Small is the gate and narrow the road that leads to life, and only a few find it' (Matthew 7:14).

Talk about

In the Lord's Prayer there is the phrase, 'Lead us not into temptation.' Sometimes it's much easier to give in to temptation and go through the wide gate than to resist temptation and choose the narrow gate, but Jesus always wants us to choose the best way.

7 Lifebelts

You will need: apples; lemon juice in a bowl; apple corers; knives; soft cheese in a tube; sliced orange cheese; cheese strings (optional)

Core an apple and carefully cut slices that are the same shape as a lifebelt. Put spare slices into the lemon juice to prevent browning. Use one apple slice as a template for cutting round a slice of orange cheese. Cut the cheese in half, then cut one half into four segments and glue them on to the apple using the soft cheese, leaving spaces between each one in a lifebelt design. Add lettering in soft cheese or cheese strings if desired, such as 'HMS St Wilf's'.

Talk about

Jesus' prayer says, 'Deliver us from evil.' It's a prayer to be rescued from evil, just as throwing a lifebelt to someone in the sea can rescue them from drowning.

8 Glory box

You will need: tiny cardboard boxes with lids on; sequins; glitter; PVA glue; spreaders

Leaving the lid on, coat the box in glue and encrust it by rolling it in the sequins or glitter or both.

Talk about

At the end of Jesus' prayer we add, 'For the kingdom, the power and the glory are yours now and forever.' This little box reminds us of the glory of God.

9 Display

You will need: the Lord's Prayer printed out in separate phrases on strips of paper; a picture of an open treasure chest; craft gems; sequins; lametta; PVA glue; spreaders

Make a display showing the open treasure chest with the Lord's Prayer phrases coming out of it like rays from a rising sun. Decorate the spaces between the phrases with gems and other sparkly stuff.

Talk about

Jesus gave us a real treasure in the special prayer he taught us.

10 Prayer candle

You will need: the Lord's Prayer printed out around the edge of a card circle; tea lights; crayons; PVA glue; spreaders; decorative bits and bobs

Glue the tea light into the centre of the circle. Colour in the lettering of the prayer and decorate the rest of the card. Make sure that no decorative bits are within reach of the candle flame and remind people never to leave the candle unattended when lit.

Talk about

Suggest that when people are at home, they could light the candle and pray the prayer together one mealtime this month.

CELEBRATION

Jesus gave his friends a brilliant present: he gave them the present of a prayer. It's a magic sort of prayer: the bigger you get, the bigger the prayer gets! Jesus' friends have been praying this prayer for nearly 2000 years and they haven't worn it out yet! We're going to learn this prayer today and see if we can say it with actions. It's a family prayer to say together, so it starts off:

Our Father in heaven **(point up with one hand and keep it up)**.

And we need reminding how holy God is, so we say that his name is holy or hallowed:

Hallowed be your name **(point up with the other hand so both arms are raised)**.

We ask God to make things better on earth, so we say:

Your kingdom come **(as you're speaking, bring your hands across your body, crossed in front of you, and then let them spread out to either side)**, *your will be done* **(continue the movement till your arms are open wide)**, *on earth* **(turn hands palms down)** *as it is in heaven* **(turn hands palms up)**.

We ask him for the good things we need:

Give us today our daily bread **(bring your hands together like a bowl in front of you)**.

And we ask him to make us right with him and with each other:

Forgive us our sins **(wipe one hand across the other twice as if wiping away dirt)**, *as we forgive those who sin against us* **(turn hands over and repeat the action four times in a rhythm with the words)**.

We ask for protection and safety:

Lead us not into temptation **(clench a fist and place one arm firmly across your chest).**
But deliver us from evil **(clench the other fist and cross that one across your chest).**

And we finish with a joyful shout of praise:

For the kingdom **(open arms wide again),** *the power* **(make a 'strong man' pose with clenched fists)** *and the glory* **(make a full circle with your hands from as high as you can to as low as you can in front of your body)** *are yours* **(push out arms forwards)** *now* **(indicate the start of a 'timeline' with your left hand)** *and forever* **(continue the timeline over to the right with a spiralling 'on and on' movement with your left hand).**
Amen! **(Finish with both arms up again and a high clap.)**

Pray it several times to practise. Try it very loud and very fast, then very quietly and with quiet music behind it. Encourage people to pray it at home at bedtime, and remind them that the older they get, the bigger the prayer will get!

Sunday treat

Forgive us our sins…

Dear Jesus, you love us so much. You want the very best for us.
You even died on the cross so that we can be forgiven!
We make mistakes and do things we know are wrong.
We're very sorry, especially for things we've done today, like… **(say your own ideas).**
Thank you that you forgive us every time we ask you to!

Take-home idea

✤ Write down two things (or more if you have time) you wish would happen. Take turns to read out your wishes.

✢ If God was making a list of what he wishes would happen, what do you think might be on it? Write down two things you think God would wish for and take turns to read them out.

Talk about what's on the lists and draw them together with a simple prayer such as: 'Our Father, thank you that you want what's good for us all. Help us to understand what you want and to do it.'

Messy team theme

✢ How much of the Lord's Prayer can you remember without help?
✢ Which part do you like best?
✢ Which part is most relevant to your Messy Church?

Our community

HOW DOES THIS SESSION HELP PEOPLE GROW IN CHRIST?

An important aspect of Messy discipleship is to serve God in the context in which he has placed us: to value the area where we live, work or go to school, and to see our role as stewards of this area. I was struck during my stay in Australia by the homage paid to the Aboriginal peoples who had been stewards of local tracts of land in the past and who were acknowledged as such in the church where we met. There was a sense of taking on responsibility for the land in a chain of heritage, something we could do well to learn from. It is good for people to have a sense of place, to celebrate their locality and to recognise the signs of God at work there in his creation and in his people. A church festival that touches on this theme is Rogationtide, which falls just before Ascension Day and is rarely celebrated these days. It used to involve beating the bounds of the parish and asking for God's blessing on the crops. Perhaps we can only make small changes, but as today's parable shows, things that start small can have a huge impact.

Main Bible story: Mark 4:30–32

ACTIVITIES

1 Moving model

You will need: sand; cornflour; water; trays

In a tray, mix four parts sand to two parts cornflour to two/three parts water to make a textured gloop. Use the gloop to model your local landscape: hills and valleys, ditches and beaches, buildings and parks. It will be solid while you model it and liquid when you stop.

Talk about
What changes have you seen in your neighbourhood recently? What changes would you like to see?

2 The interesting place where we live

You will need: cotton wool; paints; PVA glue; water; card

Shred the cotton wool and stir it up with paint, glue and a drop of water. This makes a soggy, textured modelling material that can be picked up and moulded to form a cross between a painting and a sculpture on a card base. Use it to create a representation of an interesting local landmark.

Talk about
Did you know that people in the Old Testament used to build altars around the countryside in places they felt they had met with God? The altars were piles of stones that marked the places as holy. What holy places do you know?

3 Postcards

You will need: plain postcards; postage stamps; photos of your local area printed on to paper or pictures from a local magazine; the name and address of your MP; felt-tip pens; PVA glue; spreaders

Invite everyone to put a picture on a postcard, either chopping up the photos and making collages, or using the felt-tip pens. Write the postcard to your local MP, saying what is special about the place where you live and describing what you think Messy Church adds to your community, perhaps even inviting her or him to come to a session.

Talk about

How often do you ask God to bless the government and your MP in particular? She or he has hard decisions to make every day that affect many people, and needs God's help to make the community a better place.

4 'Where I live' trays

You will need: clean, shallow, small trays like supermarket fruit trays or small shoe-box lids; home-made play dough; objects that represent something about the occupations or history of the place where you live (such as nuts and bolts for a place with an engineering industry; plastic cutlery for somewhere with a lot of restaurants; seeds, scraps of sheep's wool and tree bark for a rural area; or pictures of notable local people); metallic paint; brushes

Press the dough into the tray to make a base, then push each piece of memorabilia into the dough to make interesting patterns. Paint the whole lot with metallic paint so that you retain the different textures but achieve unity of colour.

Talk about

You are part of a heritage of people and work in the place where you live. What might you bring to your community to make it a better place? Where do you see God at work in your community?

5 Totem pole

> **You will need:** large cardboard boxes; junk-modelling materials; old magazines; or for a smaller version use tins like cocoa tins with no sharp edges and scraps of cardboard; small pieces of junk; sticky tape; paint; brushes; PVA glue; spreaders

The idea of North American totem poles was to celebrate important events and beliefs in a family's history. Choose a place, a person, an event and a memory that are important to you. Make your own totem pole, either all together or as families, to celebrate these things and people. So if school is your chosen place, you might paint a box in the colour of your uniform and place it on top of the box for Mum's office, which you've covered with cut-outs of computers and decorated with her face on one side. You might include something to represent Messy Church at the base of each one by painting the Messy splat on one side, a cross on another and stained-glass windows or something else from the place where you meet to complete the four sides.

Talk about
Why are these things and people so important to you? How do other people make your life better? How can you make life better for other people in your community or family?

6 Eggshell mosaic trees

> **You will need:** eggshells; PVA glue; acrylic paint (or ordinary paint mixed with a little PVA glue); black paper; chalk; a rolling pin

You could either do this craft as one large collaboration or as smaller, individual projects. Paint the eggshells in different colours and allow them to dry (you might want to do this before the session, or at least have some ready-painted). Either with your fingers or—more fun—with a rolling pin, gently crush the eggshells so that you have small pieces. Draw the outline of a tree in chalk on the black paper with large leaves, fruit and a nest with birds. Then spread on glue one section at a time and fill in the sections with pieces of eggshell like a mosaic. If you get bored, you can colour the rest with chalk.

Talk about

In Jesus' parable of the mustard seed the tree provides shelter and fruitfulness for the birds (hence our use of eggshells today). What do you think Jesus was really talking about?

7 Mini-golf

You will need: bricks; breeze blocks; planks; tubes and pipes large enough for a golf ball to pass through; cardboard boxes; chicken wire; golf clubs and balls

Build your own mini-golf course based on three or four local landmarks including the church building. Encourage people to design their own 'holes' using the materials provided. Then, naturally, play mini-golf.

Talk about

God made us to enjoy living on the earth he made, and these local landmarks are just a few of the wonderful things in the world to enjoy; but he also made us to enjoy living even longer in heaven. We have a lot to be thankful for.

8 Community launch pad

You will need: strong plastic cups; elastic bands; decorative scraps of paper and fabric; PVA glue; spreaders; scissors

Cut four small, equally spaced notches in the rim of a cup. Using the scraps, decorate the cup as yourself with whatever distinguishes you, leaving the notches exposed. Allow it to dry, then make one cut in each of two rubber bands and make a knot at each end. String them across the open end of the decorated cup between opposite notches so that together they form a cross. Place the decorated cup down over a plain cup to stretch the rubber bands and let it ping off.

Talk about
Your home and community and church are all like launch pads from which people jump out into the world and make it a better place. How do they help members of your family launch out?

9 Marble maze

You will need: plastic drinking straws; printouts of places and people from your community; lids from shoeboxes or similar-sized cardboard trays; marbles; PVA glue; spreaders

Glue four pictures of local places or people on the inner surface of the lid. Draw a path with right angles leading from one to another. Cut straws to go either side of this path, using the marble to check you have the right width of path, and glue them into place. Older people might want to add dead-ends and traps. Place a marble into the lid at one end of the path and tilt the lid to guide the marble down the path to 'visit' each place. You could time how long it takes people and see who can complete the course the fastest.

Talk about
It's easy to take local places for granted and forget to take time to enjoy them. Where could you go this month and be thankful that it's so near?

10 Installation tree

> **You will need:** a large sturdy cross on a base; assorted junk-modelling materials, including boxes, newspaper, cardboard tubes and margarine or ice-cream tubs; sticky tape; green paper; brown paper; feathers; scissors

Make this as big as you can. Imagine the cross as the trunk of the tree and add 'branches' to it by taping on junk such as tubes, rolled-up newspaper and opened-out boxes. Wrap the trunk and branches in brown paper and tape on leaves cut out of green paper. Make nests out of circular margarine tubs covered with brown paper scraps. Make birds out of small boxes or packets covered with feathers and tape them on to the tree.

Talk about
Often in art, Jesus' cross is shown as part of the tree of life, as out of his death came new life. Jesus is at the heart of our Messy Church, just as the cross is at the heart of this tree's ecosystem.

CELEBRATION

Show some (suitable) clips of the news, play a few moments of a recording from a children's news programme, show pictures from current affairs, or encourage people to browse through stories in newspapers, including local ones.

Sometimes we look at the news and would like to care about people in terrible situations, but it all seems too big for us. We get compassion fatigue. What difference could we possibly make to the world? We're not powerful or important. It's easier just to turn over the page or turn off the television and forget about it.

But Jesus has faith in us! He knows we can make a difference! He knows that even small people, small words and small actions can have a huge effect.

> Jesus told his friends a story. 'Imagine a seed.' *A stooge proudly and comically parades a coconut in front of everyone.* 'No, not a seed that big—a smaller seed!' *The stooge looks disappointed and parades a broad bean.* 'No, not a seed that big! A smaller seed!'

The stooge continues hamming it up, getting crosser and crosser, producing a pea, a sunflower seed, an apple pip and a poppy seed, with the leader each time encouraging everyone to join in with 'A smaller seed!' until the stooge finally mimes having a bright idea and elaborately pretends to pick up a seed like a grain of dust.

> 'Yes! That's the size of seed we mean! The smallest seed of all—a mustard seed! It's so small you can hardly see it!'

The stooge acts out the following.

> A man takes a teeny, tiny mustard seed and plants it in the ground. He waters it and weeds around it and it grows… and grows… and grows… and grows… and GROWS! Eventually it grows so big that it's the biggest plant in the whole garden—so big that birds even come and build their nests in its branches. *The stooge also enthusiastically mimes seeing the birds and pointing up at them flying, until one poops in his eye…*

Jesus wasn't just talking about gardening. He said the kingdom of heaven is like that mustard seed. It has such a tiny start, but it ends up being humungous. He was just one person, but he has been changing the world for 2000 years and he is still changing it today. So when we think we can't make a difference, let's remember that mustard seed and trust God that if we work with him to change our community for the better, he has the power to turn what we do into something HUGE!

Prayer

Spread out a map of the area and place baskets of spot stickers around the edge of it.

Let's start right now by praying tiny prayers for the place we live in. Here's a map of the place God has chosen for us to live in and here are some baskets of 'seeds'—actually sticky spots. While we play some music, I invite you to come and make a difference to our community by sticking a 'seed' over somewhere in our area that needs God's love to change it, and asking him quietly to make a difference there. It might be your own house; it might be your school or the playing field or the pub. Come with someone else and choose somewhere to pray for together.

Let's draw all these prayers together by saying the prayer of the kingdom we learned last time: the Lord's Prayer with actions (see page 93).

Sunday treat

As we forgive those who sin against us...

Dear God, we get very battered by people and things that hurt us.
Sometimes you know we feel like crumpled-up newspaper, or like punchbags, or like... **(say your own ideas).**
Those people have hurt us, but help us remember how much we hurt you without meaning to.
And help us to forgive those people, because you forgave us first.
Especially we pray for help to forgive... **(say your own ideas).**

Take-home idea

If as a family you have a regular journey through your community, pick a special feature together. It might be a tree or a telegraph pole or a street corner or a garden gnome. Agree that every time you pass it, you'll say a prayer for your town/village/street, asking God to bless the place where you live.

Messy team theme

✣ Where do you see God at work in your local community?
✣ Draw a picture of how you think the mustard tree would look if it was growing in your community.
✣ How is your Messy Church providing shelter for young and old 'birds'?

Session 8

Journeys

HOW DOES THIS SESSION HELP PEOPLE GROW IN CHRIST?

This may be a time of year when we travel on holiday or can get outside and enjoy the great outdoors more easily. This session looks at Paul's missionary journeys, introducing him as one of the key characters of the New Testament and allowing people to get to know him. His journeys and adventures across land and sea link us with the journey of the Christian life and the wide spread of the Christian church across the world, and help us to think how the kingdom of God is at work in different places. With an emphasis on space and getting wet and running about, this is a session in which we invite people to 'savour life's joys'.

Main Bible story: Paul's adventures in Acts

ACTIVITIES

1 Compass in a jam jar

You will need: sewing needles; permanent magnets; jam jars; string; paper; pencils; pens; scissors; a hole punch

Stroke the needle along its length with the magnet in the same direction as many times as you can bear in order to magnetise it. Cut a 2cm square of paper and push the needle into its centre, halfway down. Punch a hole in the paper and thread a string through. Then tie the other end of the string to the middle of a pencil so that your paper and needle dangles from it. Balance the pencil across the top of a jam jar with the needle dangling inside the jar. Wait until the needle settles and points in one direction: this is the N–S axis. Mark N-S-E-W at appropriate points on a piece of paper to sit under your jar.

Talk about
God may lead us in all sorts of directions in our lives, but, like Paul, who had to travel all over the Mediterranean, we can know he is always with us wherever he takes us.

2 Jigsaw maps

You will need: maps of the Mediterranean showing the area of Paul's missionary journeys (do an image search on the internet); card; envelopes; PVA glue; spreaders; scissors; Bibles; luggage stickers

Glue the map to the card (unless you've printed it out on card already) to strengthen it. Cut the map up into no more than 20 pieces, fewer for very young children. Decorate the envelope with luggage stickers and use it to store the jigsaw pieces. Invite someone else to put the jigsaw together.

Talk about
Try to say out loud some of the important city names on the map and point them out. You might show older people the New Testament letters that correspond to those cities. Better still, let them make the link themselves.

3 Jesus train

You will need: big and small cardboard boxes; sticky tape; cord; junk-modelling materials; scissors

Make a train: either a big one out of boxes that small people can squish themselves into, or a small one that can be pulled across a table top. Add any necessary features to the engine by taping on junk of different sorts. Consider making a thrilling opening door to a carriage by cutting into the side of a box. Link the carriages with cord.

Talk about

Just like the engine powers the carriages and takes them where they need to go, Jesus took Paul and takes us to places and people we'd never imagined.

4 Heavenly banquet

You will need: wafer cups; ice cream; jelly; sprinkles; squirty cream; sauces; sweets

Make the most delicious ice cream sundae in the world and eat it.

Talk about

At a journey's end, it's good to have a nice meal. Jesus described heaven as a place where there's a big party going on with wonderful food: perhaps even nicer food than your ice cream, if that's possible.

5 Flight

You will need: squares of paper; origami plane or bird
instructions printed from the internet or from a book

Make a bird or a paper plane. (If making the latter, you may like to
have a 'fly zone' and a 'no-fly zone' to keep people safe from well-
honed missiles.)

Talk about
Nowadays we can get on a plane, if we're rich enough, and fly
anywhere in the world. But in Paul's time—he was growing up at the
same time as Jesus—were there planes? Hovercrafts? Cars? How do
you think he travelled round to tell people about Jesus? How safe do
you think it was? Talk about the shipwreck in Acts 27—28.

6 Churches in the Bible

You will need: play dough; a large map of the Mediterranean
with towns marked as in the first century AD; a Bible; names
on cards as below; verses on cards (see page 110)

You're going to explore the idea that churches are made up of people,
and become familiar with a few of the strange place names in the New
Testament letters and in Revelation. Invite people to make a person
out of play dough. This figure represents a member of one of the
churches in the New Testament to whom Paul wrote a letter that we
still have in our Bibles today. Prepare some cards with the following
names on: Timothy, Titus and Philemon (people to whom Paul
wrote letters) and make play-dough people to represent them too.
Spread out the map on a table and put Timothy and his name card
in Ephesus (1 Timothy 1:3); Titus and his card in Crete (Titus 1:5);

and Philemon and his card in Colossae (Colossians 4:9). Depending on the age of the people participating, show them the name of a letter in the Bible and invite them to find the town or region it was written to on the map and put their person there to be a member of that church. Others might enjoy reading the verses for each church (see below), then deciding which church they want their person to belong to. There are some examples below, or you may have favourite verses from Paul's letters that you would prefer to use.

A handy mnemonic for remembering the order of some of the New Testament letters uses the order of the vowels: GAlatians, Ephesians, PhIlippians, COlossians and ThessalOnians (but pronounce the 'o' as in 'onion', which gives an 'uh' sound).

For I am convinced that neither death nor life, neither angels nor demons, neither the present nor the future, nor any powers, neither height nor depth, nor anything else in all creation, will be able to separate us from the love of God that is in Christ Jesus our Lord.
ROMANS 8:38–39

Grace and peace to you from God our Father and the Lord Jesus Christ.
1 CORINTHIANS 1:3

So you are no longer slaves, but God's children; and since you are his children, he has made you also heirs.
GALATIANS 4:7

For this reason, ever since I heard about your faith in the Lord Jesus and your love for all his people, I have not stopped giving thanks for you, remembering you in my prayers.
EPHESIANS 1:15–16

Rejoice in the Lord always. I will say it again: Rejoice!
PHILIPPIANS 4:4

*Since, then, you have been raised with Christ, set your hearts on things
above, where Christ is seated at the right hand of God.*
COLOSSIANS 3:1

*May God himself, the God of peace, sanctify you through and through.
May your whole spirit, soul and body be kept blameless at the coming
of our Lord Jesus Christ. The one who calls you is faithful, and he will
do it.*
1 THESSALONIANS 5:23–24

Talk about
Describe the early churches: how they met in people's houses, shared
their possessions, ate together and gave generously to Paul and to
other Christians in need. Think how hard it must have been to keep
believing when everyone around them believed in other gods.

7 Water painting

You will need: buckets; squeezable plastic bottles; water
pistols; water; towels

Challenge people in teams or families to draw a huge picture with
water on an outside space, such as a tarmacked or paved area, either
squirting the water or dribbling it from buckets. You could suggest
subjects that go with today's theme—for example, a letter, a ship, a
church, a tent (Paul was a tent-maker), a road, a prison or love—and
people could guess what it is they're painting.

Talk about
Give the reason for each subject and explain how it links to Paul's life.
Emphasise how much time he spent travelling by sea.

8 Envelope bridge

You will need: lots of used envelopes; sticky tape; a paddling pool or baby bath, or a strip of blue material; a football

Challenge people to build a bridge out of the envelopes that is wide and strong enough to support a football and long enough to reach across a paddling pool or baby bath of water. (If it's inside, you could even use a strip of blue material to represent the sea.) Ask people to try rolling the football across the bridge without causing it to fall into the 'sea'.

Talk about

Explain how Paul's letters crossed over sea and land to get to the people he was writing to, and how they carry the message of Jesus across the centuries to us today, like the bridge carries the football.

9 Wind-up boats

You will need: plastic bottles with lids; elastic bands; scissors

Cut the base off the bottle and cut a rectangle about 10cm x 5cm from the base end. Take this rectangle and trim its width (the side that is 5cm) by a few millimetres. Cut it in half, so that you end up with two pieces roughly 5cm by 5cm. Cut a slit in each piece, so that they will interlock with each other to make the propeller. Loop the elastic band around the bottle and fit the propeller back into the hole from which you cut it, with the elastic band stretching across it and looped over a propeller fin to hold it in place (see diagram, page 186). Turn the propeller to wind up the boat, then put it in the water to watch it move forwards on its own.

Talk about

Paul had many sea journeys, and on one he was shipwrecked, but he trusted in God and God saved him. What's the most uncomfortable thing you've ever done for God?

10 Card dolls to dress

You will need: stiff card; template of a figure; coloured and/ or patterned paper; pictures showing examples of clothes from other countries; scissors; crayons

Make a flat doll out of stiff card by drawing round the template and cutting it out. Invite people to use the coloured and patterned paper to make clothes from other countries for their doll, using the pictures as inspiration. The idea is to show how many countries around the world have Christians in them.

Talk about

Paul travelled all over the Mediterranean to tell people about Jesus. Even though we may live far away from there, Paul's travels and the travels of other Christians make it possible for us to know Jesus too. I wonder where you will go to tell people about Jesus?

CELEBRATION

Paul's missionary journeys are very complicated. After several attempts to simplify his life, I reckoned it was best to settle for a way of sharing his story that gives people a hint about who Paul was and a way into each of the letters he wrote to the different churches. So the churches won't necessarily appear in the order Paul visited them, but according to the order of their corresponding letters in the New Testament. You need a leader who can keep motivating everyone to 'row' from one church to another but who can settle people quickly to listen at each spot. The leader could also keep recapping the names of the letters in order to help people learn them without realising it.

Appoint a helper to be Paul in jail in Rome and others to be Timothy, Luke, Silas, Barnabas, Mark, Epaphras and Titus, who are all in jail with him. You'll also need seven helpers scattered around the room, each representing one of the cities or areas to which Paul sent letters (Rome, Corinth, Galatia, Ephesus, Philippi, Colossae and Thessalonica). They each need a large letter, standing for the letter Paul wrote to their church, and each needs to be ready to tell their story as below. There's no need for them to learn it word for word, just to know the gist. Someone needs to be Philemon too, and stand with the person representing Colossae.

> LEADER: Today we're going to travel around the Mediterranean Sea, so we'll need to get our rowing boats ready. *Practise rowing.* We're going to visit some of the places mentioned in the Bible, places Paul wrote letters to. But who was Paul? He can't come with us, sadly, as he's here in Rome in jail, along with some friends who also got put in prison at one time or another for following Jesus. Gentlemen, could you tell us your names?

They do so: Timothy, Luke, Silas, Barnabas, Mark, Epaphras, Titus.

> LEADER: Now, Paul, can you tell us a bit about yourself?
> PAUL: I used to hate Christians, and I loved to see them stoned to death because they didn't keep God's Law. But then I met Jesus on the road to Damascus and he came very close to me. I realised I'd been very wrong and have spent my life since telling people about Jesus and how he brings freedom.
> LEADER: Freedom? But you're in jail!
> PAUL: In Jesus I am free wherever I am. He gives freedom to all sorts of people. And I'm using my freedom to write letters that will help the Christians know Jesus better and live better lives.
> TIMOTHY: He wrote me two letters too! 1 Timothy and... um what was the other one called?
> TITUS: And he wrote one to me as well! Mine's called Titus!

PAUL: But you're not in jail in Rome: why don't you go and visit some of the churches I wrote to? You could start here in Rome if you like, down in the catacombs…

ROMAN: Paul didn't tell you he was shipwrecked on the way here and bitten by a snake! *Tell story from Acts 27:1—28:11.* He wrote the Christians here a fantastic letter—listen to my favourite bit. *Read your favourite verse from Romans.*

LEADER: That's great, but we've got a lot of other places to visit… and look, that Christian over there is waving to us. Let's leave Rome! Into your rowing boats and over the sea we go. *Repeat this with variations for each trip.*

CORINTHIAN: My name's Priscilla and here's my husband Aquila. We live here in Corinth and we're tent-makers just like Paul. He told us about Jesus. We believed in him and got baptised and Paul came to stay at our house. After he went to other places, he wrote us some great letters. Listen! *Either read your favourite verse from 1 or 2 Corinthians or use 1 Corinthians 12:12–31 to prepare for Session 15.*

GALATIAN: When Paul came here to this region of Galatia, he made a man better in Jesus' name: he made him walk again by the power of Jesus! And he wrote this brilliant bit in his letter to us. *Either choose your own verse from Galatians or use Galatians 5:22–23 to recall Session 5.*

EPHESIAN: Welcome to Ephesus! Paul didn't half create trouble here! You see, we have a local shrine and we sell a lot of silver goddesses here. But when Paul came, he stood up for Jesus and said the goddess was a load of rubbish. The silversmiths didn't sell as many statues, so they organised a riot in the city to get rid of Paul! He wrote us a fantastic letter. *Read your favourite verse from Ephesians.*

PHILIPPIAN: Paul had an exciting time here in Philippi too: he was thrown into jail for doing miracles in Jesus' name, but that night God sent an earthquake and all the prison doors burst open and everyone's chains fell off! The jailer was about to kill himself as he thought his prisoners had escaped, but Paul told him about Jesus and the jailer and all his family believed and were baptised as Christians. Then he took Paul home and gave him a slap-up meal! Here's one of my favourite bits from the letter Paul wrote to us in Philippi. *Read your favourite verse from Philippians.*

COLOSSIAN: Paul never made it here to Colossae, but he was in prison with our good friend Epaphras *(wave at Epaphras in jail)* and Epaphras learned all about Jesus from Paul and came and told us. And you should read the letter Paul wrote us. Listen to this. *Read your favourite bit from Colossians.*

PHILEMON: And my name is Philemon. I live in Colossae and Paul wrote me a letter of my very own, too!

THESSALONIAN: Paul had to run away to Athens when he came here to Thessalonica, as they rioted about what he was saying about Jesus! But the first letter he wrote to us was the first he wrote to anyone. Listen. *Read your favourite verse from 1 or 2 Thessalonians.*

LEADER *(taking everyone back to Rome)*: Paul, that's phenomenal! Did you know, we still have those letters in our Bible today? They've lasted 2000 years!

PAUL: All I want is for people to know Jesus! If you know him too, you can sing him a song with me! Let's sing together...

Prayer

Hand out postcards with a map of Paul's journeys on one side and on the other side, in nice clear writing: 'Jesus, I want to journey with you. Love from...' Invite everyone to take a prayer walk around the Mediterranean places you've just visited (in any order) as music plays, and to think about whether they would like to be on a journey with Jesus, like Paul was. You could have printouts of the special verse from each letter to collect from each place. At the end of the walk, people could sign their postcards if they want to and give them to 'Paul', who could say a gathering prayer:

Lord Jesus, thank you for inviting us on a journey with you. Help us to know you're with us wherever we go. Help us to know you more and more everywhere we go. Help us to tell everyone about you. And even if we have adventures like shipwrecks and snakes and prison and riots, let us carry on sharing your love with everyone we meet.

Sunday treat

Lead us not into temptation…

Jesus, you know what it's like to be alive and to be tempted to do bad things. There are so many temptations around us, things that turn us away from you.
Help us to be as strong as you were when you said 'no'.
Help us to be as strong in our hearts as elephants, or a dinitrogen chemical bond or… **(say your own ideas)**.

Take-home idea

Make a picture board with photos, brochures, postcards, drawings, words and so on. Place the things that you are happy or excited about on one side, and the things that you are worried or uncertain about on the other side.

Messy team theme

✤ How do you feel about journeys?
✤ Do you feel your life is a journey with God or a dead-end?
✤ How can you help each other?
✤ How can you catch the passion that Paul had for sharing the message of Jesus with others?

Session 9

Harvest

HOW DOES THIS SESSION
HELP PEOPLE GROW IN CHRIST?

Harvest is another regular festival in the church year, adapted from Old Testament harvest celebrations. Human beings have long recognised the need to give thanks for the good things that surround us and to reflect on our capacity for sharing the good things we've been given. It's a time to 'count our blessings' on our mission to share life in all its fullness and have it for ourselves. It gives people a chance to be grateful instead of grumbling, to see what they have instead of what they don't have, which is the message of a consumerist society. The story of the feeding of the 5000 puts Jesus at the heart of the celebration alongside God the Father and the work of the Spirit.

Main Bible story: John 6:5–14

You will find a great range of special Messy Church harvest crafts from Infinite Crafts to add even more variety to what you are offering: www.inf.co.uk/infinite/Messy_Church_Craft_Kits.html.

ACTIVITIES

1 Jigsaw puzzle

You will need: squares of stiff card about 20cm x 20cm; nature-themed stickers; clear plastic covering film (optional); scissors; felt tip pens

Decorate your square with the stickers and add more details if you want with felt-tips. Cover with film if using. Cut the square into four smaller squares or six smaller rectangles and invite a small person to make the jigsaw up again and see the bigger picture.

Talk about
What in the world makes you thank God?

2 Funky storage tubes

You will need: crisp tubes or tubs, whisky tubes or similar; food magazines; vintage food magazines if possible; scissors; watered-down PVA glue; brushes

Older people may prefer to cover their tube with vintage food magazines while younger people may opt for modern, brightly coloured ones. Cut the magazine pages into strips about 4cm wide and glue them either lengthways or horizontally to overlap each other and cover the tube. Cut out letters from the magazines to say 'All good gifts' and stick those around the tin. Choose a particularly striking picture and cut it out carefully to glue on to the lid. Brush over with a coat of watery PVA glue to give a gloss. Small-sized crisp tubs are also handy and fun to cover.

Talk about
How do you say thank you for the good gifts around us in the world? Do you know the harvest song this comes from? 'All good gifts around us are sent from heaven above. Then thank the Lord, oh thank the Lord, for all his love' ('We Plough the Fields and Scatter'; words by Matthias Claudius, translated by Jane M. Campbell).

3 Storytellers

You will need: used envelopes with plastic windows in; strips of card; pens; scissors; sticky tape

Slit open the envelope at both ends. On a strip of card about 30cm long, draw a storyboard or cartoon strip of the story of the feeding of the 5000 from right to left. The stages might be: 1) Jesus and his friends on a mountain relaxing; 2) crowds coming to see him; 3) Jesus asking Philip where to buy bread for them; 4) Philip rolling around in laughter at such a silly question; 5) the boy with his lunch; 6) Jesus blessing the lunch; 7) everyone eating to their heart's content; 8) the twelve baskets of leftovers.

Decorate the front of the envelope with a good title for the story. Push the cartoon strip in one end of the envelope and tell the story as each part of it passes behind the window.

Talk about
Tell the story to me.

4 Whipping cream

You will need: whipping cream; hand whisk or rotary whisk; bowl; scones; jam

Whip the cream until it's stiff, then spread jam on a scone and add your own hand-whipped cream. (You could also try making your own butter with double cream shaken in a jar for ten minutes, but it's very strenuous and doesn't always work.)

Talk about
Many people are involved in making our food for us. Are we ever thankful for their care and professionalism?

5 Picnic seat

You will need: self-sealing plastic bags; paper to fit inside the bags; magazine pictures of bread and fish; bubble wrap; PVA glue; spreaders; scissors

Decorate the paper with a collage of bread and fish. Insert it into the bag face up and loosely stuff the bag behind the picture with bubble-wrap strips or scrunched up pieces. (If you're feeling green you could use old disembowelled jiffy bags.) Seal the bag and try sitting on it.

Talk about
Jesus and his friends and the crowds had a fantastic picnic on the hillside, all because one boy was generous with the little he had and Jesus had the power to make it into something huge.

6 Five thousand people!

You will need: potato stamps carved into people, or other people stamps; paint; huge sheets of paper; a tally chart

Draw Jesus and the little boy from the story in the centre of the paper. Invite everyone to add as many people stampings as they can to get the total up to 5000. They should keep count of how many they have stamped all over the sheet of paper and tell you so that you can add it to the running total on the tally chart.

Talk about
Even if we got to 5000, there were still more people that Jesus fed, as this number didn't include the women and children! Isn't Jesus amazing?

7 Print on cloth

You will need: cloth to print on: fabric bags, if money permits, or hankies, tea towels, T-shirts or similar; apples; fabric paint in trays

Print an apple design on the fabric as a reminder of the good things all around us as the apple harvest is brought in.

Talk about

What are your favourite fruits? If you had to go and live on another planet, what foods would you miss most?

8 Apple harvest

You will need: apples; an apple press if possible or ingredients for recipes involving apples

If you have access to an apple press, it would be great fun to make apple juice from everyone's spare apples. If not, make the most of the harvest by having a cooking session to make apple pies, apple chutney or apple cake.

Talk about

Isn't it fun and cheap to make use of seasonal ingredients? How much do we need to have before we feel we have enough to give some away to other people?

9 Edible lunch basket

You will need: small, plain pretzels; fizzy fish sweets; good-quality puffy rolls (not flat ones); knives

Hollow out the roll to make the basket. Older people could carefully leave a bread handle if desired, picking out the bread underneath it. In the hollow, put five pretzels to represent the loaves and two fizzy fish.

Talk about
How easy is it to share what we have, even if we were given it as a gift in the first place?

10 Great food challenge

You will need: an atlas; lots of groceries; outline of a world map on a large sheet of paper; paint in various colours; paint brushes

Choose a food item that you sometimes have at home. Look up on its packet where it comes from. Use the atlas if necessary to find out where that is and paint in that country on the map. If it is already painted in, add some dots in a different colour on top of the first colour. As you paint, say thank you to God for the people who grew that food for you.

Talk about
Isn't it amazing that we can eat food that has come from so many different places!

CELEBRATION

In this story, where you need the characters to speak, you say the words and let them repeat them.

In our special kingdom prayer, do you remember the part of the prayer about food? That's right: we pray, 'Give us today our daily bread.' We don't take our food for granted: we're grateful to God for giving it to us. Jesus always remembered to thank God for his food because he thought about God the whole time. Do you remember the famous story about Jesus out in the countryside with his friends?

Let's have someone to be Jesus, Philip and Andrew.

Jesus looked up and saw a great crowd coming towards him. *Can you all go to the back, then come forward to stand in this space here, like the crowd coming as close as they could to Jesus?* Be as quiet as you can! Jesus might be about to say something fantastic and you don't want to miss it!

And when Jesus saw all these people, he said to Philip, 'Where shall we buy bread for these people to eat?' Philip looked at the thousands of people and said, 'It would take almost a year's wages to buy enough bread for each one to have a bite!'

Now we need a boy to come and bring this lunchbox to Andrew.

But a small boy was talking to another of Jesus' friends—Andrew. And Andrew said to Jesus, 'Here is a boy with five small barley loaves and two small fish, but how far will they go among so many?'

Jesus said, 'Have the people sit down.' There was plenty of grass in that place, and they sat down. About 5000 men were there, plus women and children—a lot of people! *Andrew and Philip get everyone sitting down.* Jesus then took the food, said thank you to God (*or use your usual Messy Church grace*), and gave out the bread and the fish to everyone (*mime passing the food to each other*) until everyone had had enough! *Let's pat those full tummies…*

124

Then Jesus said to his disciples, 'Gather the pieces that are left over. Let nothing be wasted.' *Can you help collect up all the bits?* So they gathered them and filled twelve baskets with leftovers! They were all amazed at what Jesus could do.

Just like the time when the tiny mustard seed became a huge tree, Jesus took the tiny lunch and transformed it into a huge feast. What an amazing God we have!

Prayer

You can either say the words in bold or simply demonstrate them and encourage people to copy you. For our prayers today we're thinking about what we have been given and what we do with it.

Can you imagine you're holding something tiny in your hands?
Lord Jesus, like the little boy with his lunch, we don't have very much.
Now open your hands as if they're empty.
But we have more than those who have nothing at all.
Now go back to holding something tiny.
And we thank you for what you have given us.
Hold your hands up towards God.
We know when we give something to you.
Bring your hands down and offer them out in front of you.
You can turn something tiny into something huge.
Spread out your arms in an expansive gesture.
So that everyone in our world has enough.
Hold out your hands as if they're full of a lovely present.
Thank you, God. Amen.

Sunday treat

But deliver us from evil...

Jesus, you are with us wherever we go, like a shepherd looking after his sheep. When we are in danger, please rescue us.

You are our superhero, stronger than..., faster than..., more powerful than..., better than..., kinder than... **(say your own ideas)**.

Take-home idea

Harvest is a time when we can thank God for the good things we have. Often, we gather food to give to others to thank God for the food he has provided for us. Place an apple, a banana, a lemon and some grapes on a plate in the centre of the dining table. Use the fruit as a way into prayer as a family.

✛ Apples—could remind us to pray for making the right choice when faced by temptation. This links to the Bible story of Adam and Eve when they disobeyed God by eating the fruit (traditionally an apple) that they should not have eaten.
✛ Bananas—could help us to pray for justice for those who are suffering because of the unfair trade laws of our world. This links to the fact that many of the bananas now available in the supermarket are fairtrade. This means the people who produce them get the right amount of money for them.
✛ Lemons—could help us to think of those who are facing hard and bitter times. Lemons and lemon juice are very sharp and sour, which reminds us of the sourness some people face in their lives.
✛ Grapes—could help us to pray for those who have things to celebrate at this time. Grapes and wine were often used, and still are, as part of a celebration.

Jesus said: 'You did not choose me. I chose you and sent you out to produce fruit, the kind of fruit that will last' (John 15:16, CEV).

Messy team theme

✛ In what ways do you see the story of the feeding of the 5000 happening in your Messy Church?
✛ How does it leave you feeling about Jesus?
✛ How much of the praise goes to him in your Messy Church?

Session 10

Light up the darkness

HOW DOES THIS SESSION
HELP PEOPLE GROW IN CHRIST?

There are mixed opinions about Hallowe'en celebrations. Some see them as unwholesome at the very least, while others see them as harmless fun. A growing number of Messy Churches want to offer a fun celebration for their families at this time of year, but without the glorification of darkness and horror. So this session concentrates on the theme of light in the darkness, rather than darkness taking over the light. It offers a positive alternative, rather than a blanket 'Christians don't do Hallowe'en,' which is a hard message for children faced with the prospect of missing out on all the fun that their friends are having. After all, the Christian life is about saying 'yes' a hundred times more often than saying 'no'. Many churches invite everyone to come dressed as their favourite superhero/heroine for the occasion. We've linked the theme of light with the biblical idea of God's word being 'a light for my path' (Psalm 119:105) to give us a chance to celebrate God's present of the Bible as well.

Main Bible story: Luke 11:33

ACTIVITIES

1 Illuminated initial

You will need: examples of illuminated manuscript initials; colouring-in sheets of initials (available free online—do a search on 'illuminated initial to colour'); paints/felt-tip pens; calligraphy pen and ink

Describe how the medieval monks wanted their copies of the Bible to be the most beautiful pieces of work they could produce, so that everyone would see how precious God's word is. Invite people to find their own initial to colour. Older people might like to use a concordance to find a word or verse in the Bible that starts with that letter to write next to it in calligraphy. Younger people might simply write their name, followed by 'is loved by Jesus'.

Talk about
One of the psalms says, 'Your word is a lamp to my feet and a light for my path' (Psalm 119:105), which is why we're making this as colourful as we can. Do you ever use the stories in the Bible to help you make decisions?

2 Sweet Bible scrolls

You will need: fondant icing (or marzipan—but check for nut allergies); cocktail sticks; dolly mixtures or similar small sweets; black and yellow writing icing or icing in a squeezable tube; Bible verses on cards as below

Roll out a thin rectangle of icing or marzipan to about 8cm x 4cm. Write on it in icing all or a part of your favourite verse about light.

such as 'Let there be light' (Genesis 1:3); 'My God turns my darkness into light' (Psalm 18:28); 'Let us walk in the light of the Lord' (Isaiah 2:5); 'Arise, shine, for your light has come' (Isaiah 60:1); 'The light shines in the darkness' (John 1:5); 'I am the light of the world' (John 9:5); 'The light of the gospel' (2 Corinthians 4:4); 'You are all children of the light' (1 Thessalonians 5:5); 'God is light; in him there is no darkness at all' (1 John 1:5). Put a sweet on the end of each cocktail stick and place one at each end of the rectangle as the handles of the scroll. Then either roll it up and eat it (avoiding the sticks) or put it on a paper plate and paint with yellow icing some rays streaming out from the scroll as if it's shining like a light.

Talk about
Why have you chosen this verse or word? Why is it special to you? How do you feel about the Bible?

3 Light me!

You will need: lining paper or wallpaper; pencils; bright paints; glitter; 'whiter than white' washing powder and a 'black light' or UV light (optional)

Lie on the paper in a wild position and get a friend to draw around your outline. Then you draw round them on their piece of paper. Paint the inside of the outline as brightly as you can. Throw on handfuls of glitter to stick to the wet paint. You have made a bright 'me' full of light and life and colour.

If you want to add another dimension, mix some washing powder (the sort that promises to make your whites whiter than white) with water to make a paint consistency and paint around the outline with this. In a dark room, use the UV light to make it glow.

Talk about
How can you shine for God in your everyday life? What can you do to

bring light to others? Do you know anyone who is full of light? What are they like?

4 Banish the darkness

You will need: milk; bowl; various food colourings; washing-up liquid or liquid soap; cotton buds or cotton-wool balls

Put some milk into a bowl and drop a few drops of different food colourings on to it. Dip both ends of a cotton bud into washing-up liquid or liquid soap and drop it on to the surface of the milk. Watch the way the detergent changes the colours.

Talk about
The soap pushes the colours away; when light comes into darkness it works in a similar way and pushes the darkness away. Can you think of any ways of bringing Jesus' light into your work or school?

5 Lantern

You will need: clear glass jars with lids; stickers; fluorescent card; glue; the very thin glow-sticks that are used for bracelets; string; pens

Draw round the lid of your jar on to the fluorescent card and cut out the circle. Decorate it with pens or stickers. Glue it on to the lid of the jar. Attach a string handle to carry it by. Stuff two or three glow-sticks into the jar, so that they 'snap' (follow the manufacturer's instructions) and start to glow. Screw on the lid and turn out the lights.

Talk about

The glow-sticks have to be 'broken' before they can shine out fully. Can you think of someone who was broken so that his light would shine out to the whole world?

6 Mobiles

You will need: fluorescent card; transparent thread; whisky tube, crisp tube or similar; normal thread; templates of smiley faces, candle, lighthouse, torch, star, sun, moon and any other shapes to represent light; shiny stickers; dark paper; luminous paint (optional); scissors; PVA glue; spreaders; pens; a hole punch

Cover the tube in dark paper and decorate it with stickers. Use the smiley face templates to draw three to five shapes on the fluorescent card, then cut these out in a double thickness of card. Paint the edges with luminous paint if using, glue the identical pairs together so that they're double-sided and punch a hole in the top of each one. Thread them on to transparent thread and tie the threads on to the horizontal tube so that the shapes hang below. Use the normal thread to hang the mobile.

Talk about
There are many different sorts of light in the world. What do each of these do? Which is most like the sort of light that Jesus brings?

7 Stained-glass windows

You will need: greaseproof paper; printouts of simple outlines (flower, planet, star, rocket, letters of the alphabet); old wax crayons in various colours; a grater; an iron; an ironing board; cloth; sequins (optional); PVA glue; thread

Grate the crayons so that you have shavings of different colours. Put your chosen outline on the ironing board. Place a piece of greaseproof paper over the design outline and sprinkle the shavings sparingly inside the outline. Place another piece of greaseproof paper over the top and let someone responsible iron over it very gently and briefly with a warm iron until the shavings melt together. Allow this to set and then peel off the greaseproof paper. If the layer of wax is too thin to peel off the paper, simply leave the wax layer on the paper and cut the shape out of wax and paper with scissors—but if you let it cool enough it will probably peel off happily on its own. Add sequins if desired. Hang up in a window on a thread.

Talk about
One definition of a saint is that they are a person the light shines through. Are you that sort of person?

8 Swinging comet

You will need: paper that is easy to scrunch up; white or yellow carrier bags or bin bags; elastic bands; string (glow-in-the-dark laces if you can find them); scissors

Scrunch the paper into a ball about the size of a tennis ball. Turn the bag inside out if there is print on the outside and push the ball of paper into it to wrap it, and then fasten it with the elastic band, leaving the upper end of the bag free. Cut the upper end of the bag into strips to make the tail of the comet. Tie a string 'lead' around the elastic band and attach the laces (if using) to add to the effect of the tail. Hold it by the string and swing it around or pull it behind you like a kite.

Talk about
How many people can you show your comet to? Jesus wants us to share his message of light and love in the same way, not keeping it hidden but showing it to other people.

9 Morse Code

You will need: torches; a copy of the Morse Code; pens; paper

Stand at the opposite end of the room from your friend or relative and use the torch to flash a short message in Morse Code to them, like 'Hi' or 'U R Great' (older ones could use text spellings to keep it shorter). See if you can understand your partner. Write down the letters if necessary. Younger people may enjoy just echoing back the number of flashes you make at them.

Talk about
God sends his message down the centuries with words in the Bible, and they still light up people's lives.

10 Mad hat

You will need: long, glittery pipe cleaners, cheap headbands or lengths of wide elastic to fit round heads; cut-outs of stars from fluorescent card; glow-sticks; anything else sparkly to decorate with

Give each person a headband and free rein with the other articles you have and invite them to make the maddest hat or headgear they can.

Talk about
Jesus said that we should shine our lights out in the open where they can be seen, making us just as visible as these hats. What do you think he means?

CELEBRATION

Say: 'None of you lights a lamp and puts it in a place where it will be hidden, or under a bowl. Instead you put it on its stand, so that those who come in may see the light' (Luke 11:33).

Encourage lots of audience participation in the following as you try to put the light in lots of ridiculous places, including under a bowl or basket. Practise beforehand with a stooge who can mime the actions for you as below.

It's very dark in here, isn't it? But it doesn't matter, as I have a brilliant light. Here it is! Now, where would be the best place to put it? Ah, here! No? Well, how about here? No? Here is a good place! Well, where *should* I put it? Why?

You're absolutely right: a light's no good hidden away, is it? If you've got a light, you need to make sure everyone can see it or they might fall over (*stooge trips up*) or bump into things (*stooge pretends to*) or fall into enormous deep holes (*stooge mimes this*).

Jesus said, 'I am the light of the world' (John 8:12). He wants his light to shine in every single one of us. He doesn't want that light to be hidden away: he wants us to show his love and goodness and care to everyone around us. And God gave us his special book, the Bible, to help us as we try to shine like Jesus does. Someone here who I think is really good at doing that is… (*add name*) and I've asked him/her to tell us all what they do to shine Jesus' light to other people.

Invite a pre-warned person from the congregation to come and talk briefly about the way they show love and care for people around them, how the Bible inspires them and how Jesus is glorified through this.

Jesus invites us all to shine for him in different ways. I wonder how you shine his light out to others? You might not realise you do it. Ask the person you came with if they think you shine for Jesus.

Prayer

Set up a wooden cross lying flat in a sand tray and baskets of tea lights within easy access. Have several responsible people with tapers and plenty of supervision.

One tiny light can make a huge difference. Let's see what a difference many lights shining can make. Here's a cross that stands for the pain of the world and all the things that are dark and hurtful in it. Come and light a candle and place it on the cross and ask Jesus to show you how to shine for him in dark places.

Sunday treat

For the kingdom, the power and the glory are yours, now and forever.

God, you are bigger than everything and everyone.
You were there in the beginning and you go on forever without an end.
We love you more than… (say your own ideas).
Help us to love you more every day of this week.

Take-home idea

This month, try to read a short story from a children's version of the Bible every day and enjoy the way Jesus shines through the words.

Messy team theme

✣ Do you see yourselves as giving families a good time or standing up against the forces of evil?
✣ How rooted are you at the moment in the light of God's word?
✣ How can you encourage each other to read the Bible?

Session 11

Remember me

HOW DOES THIS SESSION
HELP PEOPLE GROW IN CHRIST?

This session may come at a time of year when we remember those who have died in the service of their country. In the UK, Remembrance Day, with its associated poppies and respect for the armed forces, has grown hugely in recent years and makes up a very significant part of the national heritage. The Christian themes of self-sacrifice, service, death and the promise of heaven weave themselves around this time of year. Remembering what our soldiers have offered also links to a possible Communion service that includes a time to remember Jesus' offering of himself. We think about what 'practising acts of kindness' means in its fullest sense. Any fireworks that we might want to include could be seen as symbols of the glorious resurrection that followed Jesus' act of ultimate sacrifice.

Main Bible story: Luke 23:32–43

ACTIVITIES

---

1 Funky bracelet

You will need: thin, circular pieces of funky foam in red, green and black; big needles; threading elastic (the very thin, stringy sort); hole punches; pony beads; scissors

Have a happy time punching out lots of holes from the funky foam: this in itself is rather good fun. Use the big needle, threaded with elastic, to link the resulting little circles together to make a bracelet. You can either add a few circles and space them with pony beads or you can add lots and make a very smart bracelet on which the circles are tightly compressed.

Talk about
The bracelet is in the colours of the Remembrance Day poppies to remind us of the people who have given up their lives for others. What qualities do you need as a person to be able to give up your life for others? Which of those qualities did Jesus have when he chose to go to the cross for us? (Remember that some families may have lost a family member in action.)

2 Bubbles

You will need: water; glycerine; good-quality washing-up liquid; bubble wands; wire loops; bowls; floor covering; towels

Mix up some bubble mixture in a bowl using one part washing-up liquid to ten parts water plus a little glycerine, depending on the hardness of your water. Have fun blowing bubbles and playing with the different sizes from different wands.

Talk about
A bubble lasts only for a few seconds, but the memories of people we love usually remain for our whole lives. What sorts of things do we do to remember people we love? What did Jesus invite his friends to do to remember him? On the cross, one of the other men crucified with Jesus asked Jesus to remember him. Can God ever forget us?

3 Foil cross

You will need: thick (corrugated) card; tinfoil, foil wrappers from chocolates (alas, this may involve some team eating beforehand) or posh foil from a craft shop; different coloured card circles about 3–4cm in diameter; ballpoint pens; PVA glue; spreaders; sticky tape; safety pins

Smooth the foil out over the thick card, shiny side down. Gently draw a cross shape (about 3–4cm high) on it with the ballpoint pen, then gradually press harder and harder with the pen over the outline until it 'cuts itself out'. Turn over the remaining foil and glue it on to a card circle in a contrasting colour to make a badge. The card colour should show through the cross-shaped hole. Tape the safety pin on behind.

Talk about

Christians remember what Jesus did in his life through telling stories and coming to church. In churches there are objects like crosses to help us remember, and Christians celebrate Jesus' death and coming back to life with a special meal. We remember what happened in the past, but because Jesus came back to life, we can look forward to all the things he's still going to do in the future.

4 String art frame

You will need: for younger ones, a paper plate with a circle about 8cm in diameter drawn centrally on it and 24 notches cut into the outer edge at regular intervals; for older people, a rectangle of strong, stiff card; wool and embroidery silks in various colours; sticky tape; a digital camera and printer for instant photos (ideally, but people could take photos and print them at home)

Younger people should attach a piece of wool or embroidery silk to one notch in their paper plate, then count five notches round and pass the wool through this notch, then count another five notches round and so on. This should create a web of wool around the edge of the plate, leaving the central circle clear. They can paste a photo of someone special to them into the circle.

Older people should use scissors to make a shallow notch in the cardboard either side of each corner of the frame (eight notches in total). Each notch should be no further than a third of the length of the side from the corner. Then take the wool or silk and make a geometric pattern across from one side to its opposite, experimenting with the pattern made by using different notches from one edge to another (see diagram, page 187). You should end up with a web over each corner. Secure each end by tying or with a small piece of tape and put a photo in the centre.

Talk about
We have pictures to remind us of people we love, and some churches contain pictures of Jesus to remind the congregation of different parts of his life. Other churches remember Jesus through symbols or words.

5 Electric maze

You will need: an electric maze, made beforehand using instructions from the internet; blindfolds; prizes

Make a simple electric maze from instructions on a website (such as www.ehow.com/how_8677202_create-circuit-maze-elementary-school.html or www.teachengineering.org/view_activity.php?url =collection/wpi_/activities/wpi_wire_maze/wpi_maze_joy_act.xml) and check it works safely.

Holding the U-shaped loop by the insulated wire, guide it over the wobbly wire. If you touch the wobbly wire with the loop, the circuit should be completed and the bulb should light up. (You could use a buzzer, but some children find these alarming.)

Use the maze as a memory test: move the U-shaped loop from one end of the wobbly line to the other without touching it and making it light up. Make the loop bigger if it's too hard. Do this a few times until you succeed. Then try it blindfolded: can you *remember* the shape of the maze? Prizes may be in order (and consolation prizes).

Talk about

How easy is it to remember? Do you get pictures in your head? Different people remember in different ways. When you go into the celebration, think about what you can see around you that reminds you of something else.

6 Clothes-peg catapult

You will need: wire-spring clothes pegs; blocks of wood for bases; thin sticks of soft wood about 10cm long, like lolly sticks (or very thick card); elastic bands; mini foil apple pie dishes; drawing pins or tacks; hammer; balls of tissue paper; target

Make a catapult by laying the clothes peg on the base so that you can still press it open, and attaching it with plenty of elastic bands. (A glue gun is an ideal way of fixing it, but this is dangerous and needs to be done by an adult, which takes half the fun out of it.) Attach the foil dish to the lolly stick about 3cm away from one end, using a drawing pin or tack. A grown-up should use the hammer to tap the end of the pin back against the stick on the opposite side. Attach the wooden stick to the top edge of the clothes peg, again with elastic bands or a glue gun. Place a tissue-paper ball in the dish, press down on the lolly stick and fire the ball at the target. If you prefer, leave out all the materials and invite people to invent their own catapults.

Talk about

When you press down on the handle of the catapult, you're building up a load of potential energy inside it. We can use our own potential energy in different ways. What sorts of things can we do to use all that energy for peace, not war?

7 Rosemary crushing

You will need: lots of fresh rosemary (someone somewhere will have it in their garden); mortars and pestles; cotton buds

Break the rosemary into little twigs and crush it using the mortars and pestles. You can use the oil (if you manage to produce any, which would take an awful lot of effort) to flavour breadsticks, to put in water to rinse brown hair and give it a shine, or to dab on your temples if you have a headache. But mostly this is about the fun of pounding something into a pulp and smelling it. Use the cotton buds to soak up the oil and take it home if desired.

Talk about

Rosemary is traditionally a symbol of remembering. Take a good smell of it; perhaps one day the smell of rosemary will remind you of Messy Church!

8 Latin American-style cross

You will need: crosses drawn out on card or paper and divided into five sections; felt-tip pens or paints; black marker pens; a few examples of Latin American crosses

Decorate a cross to show the Good Friday narrative from Luke 23:32–48, drawing a simple picture or symbol from each part of the story in each of the sections: the three men on the crosses; rolling the dice for Jesus' belongings; mocking faces; vinegar; paradise. Outline the colours in black marker if you want to.

Talk about
Tell the story of Jesus' death on the cross from the pictures on your cross.

9 Dice

You will need: nets of dice (search online for 'dice net'— there are even free ways to generate and print a word on each face of the dice); sticky tape or PVA glue; felt-tip pens

Cut out your net of the dice and decorate each face so that it features someone to remember in your prayers this week. You might just write their name, or one member of the family could write while another draws.

Talk about
When might you roll your dice this week? At breakfast time? At bedtime? Ask God to bless the person who shows on top when you roll the dice.

10 Picturing paradise

You will need: very thin sweet laces such as liquorice or apple laces; any sweets that could become flowers or plants or trees, such as chocolate buttons with dolly mixture petals, cola bottle tree trunks with green icing leaves, foam banana petals, liquorice allsorts flowers with green lace stalks or sherbet pip grass; biscuits; icing

Jesus said to the criminal, 'Today you will be with me in paradise' (Luke 23:43). Explain that 2000 years ago, people thought of paradise as a beautiful garden. Divide your biscuit into quarters with the laces to make a garden with four flower beds, and 'plant' a different sweet plant or flower in each quarter.

Talk about

Perhaps Jesus was inviting the criminal on the cross to come and walk in a beautiful garden on the other side of death, just like God walked with Adam and Eve in the Garden of Eden before death even existed.

CELEBRATION

This session on remembering is a good opportunity to think about Jesus' death and celebrate his coming back to life. The whole celebration is woven into the meal around the tables and requires some rehearsal by the core team. You'll need a 'host' for each table who can keep everyone engaged and enthused, and the props and scripts should be prepared beforehand. These are designed for seven tables, but change this to suit your numbers. You will need to give each reader a copy of the script for that narrative with their own line highlighted so that they know what their cue is.

Each table should have

1) three questions for the youngest people at their table (see page 144);
2) an object for the crucifixion narrative (either a sword, crown of thorns, robe, nails, cross, dice or grave clothes);
3) the script for the crucifixion narrative (see page 145);
4) the script for the resurrection narrative (see page 146).

At your table:

Work together to set your table, having fetched a tray with the following on it: tablecloths, candlestick and candle, matches, flowers, plates, cutlery, cups plus one spare cup, grape juice, mini breadsticks, pots of horseradish, apple mush and salt water. The host at each table gives out the different parts (questions 1, 2 and 3 to the three youngest people; the object for the crucifixion narrative to someone else; a line of script from the crucifixion narrative to a confident reader; and a line of script from the resurrection narrative to one of the women). Hosts should try to be natural, not read every single word from the script.

HOST: Now who has the first question?
CHILD 1: Why have we got this funny food on the table?
HOST: The food helps us remember the miserable time the Hebrew people had in Egypt long, long ago. Pass round the horseradish: this is bitter and they felt bitter at being kept as slaves. Pass round the salt water: this is for the tears they cried because life was so hard. Pass round the apple mush. This is for the mud they mixed with straw to make bricks for the pyramids.

Now who has the second question?
CHILD 2: Did they stay slaves forever?
HOST: No! God rescued them and brought them out of Egypt, through the Red Sea and into freedom in the Promised Land. And God's people remember that rescue in a special meal. So we can celebrate that salvation with a toast. To freedom!
ALL: To freedom!

HOST: Who has the third question?
CHILD 3: Why have we got bread and wine on the table?
HOST: Because when Jesus was sharing this special meal with his friends, the night before he died, he changed the meal. He broke the bread and gave it to them saying, 'This is my body, broken for you. Do this to remember me.' *Pass round the bread.* And he took the wine and said, 'This is my blood, poured out for you. Do this to remember me.' *Pass round the grape juice.* Jesus was going to rescue everyone and free them from everything that cut them off from God. People who follow Jesus remember that rescue with a special meal.
And now we're going to have our meal before we hear the next part of the story.

Bring the first course, serve it and eat. Have a signal for everyone to pay attention to the next part, which takes place in the centre of the tables: some music playing, for example. Encourage the person from your table with the object to bring it to the centre when it is mentioned (see bold text). The first reader begins:

READER 1: After the meal, Jesus and his friends went to the Garden of Gethsemane. Jesus prayed while his friends went to sleep.

READER 2: Then in the dark, a crowd of soldiers with **swords** came to arrest Jesus. All his friends ran away. Peter followed in secret to see what would happen.

READER 3: When someone accused Peter of being one of Jesus' friends, Peter was so scared, he said he didn't know Jesus at all.

READER 4: Jesus was put on trial and found guilty of saying that he was the Son of God. So they whipped him and put a **crown of thorns** on his head and an emperor's **robe** on him to make fun of him. Then they took him outside the city to be crucified. By now it was Good Friday.

READER 5: They **nailed** him to a **cross**. While he was dying, the soldiers played **dice** to see who would win his clothes.

READER 6: One of the criminals who was also being crucified was mean to Jesus, but the other one said Jesus had done nothing wrong. He said to Jesus, 'Remember me when you come into your kingdom.' Jesus said, 'Truly I tell you, today you will be with me in paradise.'

READER 7: At the end Jesus said, 'Father, into your hands I commit my spirit.' And he died. They wrapped his body in **grave clothes**. A man called Joseph took his body to a tomb that had been cut out of the rock. They rolled a heavy stone over the entrance to the tomb and went away to wait until the Sabbath was over.

The team carry all the objects into an area designated as the tomb during the following singing:

SONG: 'Jesus, remember me when you come into your kingdom' (Taizé chant).

LEADER: On Easter Sunday, early in the morning, a strange thing happened. The women got up very early and came to the tomb. *The women from each table with script lines come to the tomb and look inside.*
WOMAN 1: We went to the tomb to put spices on Jesus' body.
WOMAN 2: We wondered how we would manage to roll away the stone, as it was so heavy.
WOMAN 3: But when we got to the tomb we were amazed.
WOMAN 4: The stone had been rolled away!
WOMAN 5: Jesus' body had gone!
WOMAN 6: There were only his grave clothes left!
WOMAN 7: And we met an angel who said Jesus is ALIVE!
LEADER: And they went and told everyone they met. And many people met the living Jesus. He had certainly died, but now he had come back to life! Through his death on the cross he set us free from the power of death so that anyone who believes in him is free to live forever too. Let's drink a final toast to freedom!
ALL: To freedom! *(Get out some party poppers and pop them.)*

LEADER: And now to finish our celebration meal, let's pray for each other in the words of the Messy Grace, before we have our cake!

May the grace of our Lord Jesus Christ **(hold out your hands as if expecting a present)**
And the love of God **(put your hands on your heart)**
And the fellowship of the Holy Spirit **(hold hands)**
Be with us all now and for ever. Amen! **(Raise hands together on the word 'Amen'.)**

Sunday treat

May the grace of our Lord Jesus Christ…

Thank you, Jesus, for your grace to us.
Thank you for your generosity.
Thank you for all you give us and forgive us for.
Thank you especially for... **(say your own ideas)**.

Take-home idea

✣ How good is your memory?
✣ Who has the best memory in your family?

Play a 'remembering tray' game together. Choose between six and ten items depending on the age of your children. Include a photo of someone you all know as one of the items. Place all the items on a tray. Allow everyone one minute to look at the items to remember them. Then cover the tray with a towel or cloth. Each person then has a minute (or longer for younger ones) to write down (or say if they are too young to write) what was on the tray.

✣ How many can each person remember?

Now take the photo and ask each person:

✣ What is your main memory of the person in the photo?
✣ Is he or she funny, kind, gentle, brave...?

Now ask if anyone can think of someone they know who is brave or is involved in a war somewhere in the world.

Remembrance Sunday is a time to remember those who have been very brave and fought in wars. Take time to say thank you to God for people who fought in defence of their country in the wars of the past or who are fighting now. Pray for those who have lost friends and family they loved in a war. Maybe you could write a prayer together as a family or read the following prayer together:

Lord God, we thank you for the many men and women who fought in defence of their country in the past and for those who still do today. Please be with them and their families and friends. We pray for those people

who have lost friends and family they loved in a war. Please bring comfort to them. We pray for peace for the friends and families of people involved in wars now. We pray that they will know that you are with them.
We pray this in Jesus' name. Amen.

Messy team theme

✛ Of all the people mentioned in the Good Friday story, who do you most identify with and why?
✛ Which person in your team do you consider the most self-sacrificing?
✛ What is your fondest memory of your time at Messy Church?

Christmas

HOW DOES THIS SESSION HELP PEOPLE GROW IN CHRIST?

Christmas is part of our seasonal celebration of the major stories of the Christian faith. We remind everyone that Christ is at the heart of Christmas and keep his story alive among the tinsel and turkey. Yes, Christmas features in both the earlier Messy Church books as well as *Messy Christmas*, but it comes round every year and is a huge opportunity for family celebration.

Main Bible story: Luke 1—2

You will find a great range of special Messy Church Christmas crafts from Infinite Crafts to add even more variety to what you are offering: www.inf.co.uk/infinite/Messy_Church_Craft_Kits.html.

ACTIVITIES

1 Angelic host picture

You will need: sturdy card backing; clear plastic bottles; tinsel, lametta or shredded foil; card; dark-blue paint; paint brushes; yellow or white paint (optional); glittery pipe cleaners; felt-tip pens; paper ovals in different skin colours; scissors; sticky tape; thread

This craft is 3D, so may need to be hung up rather than pinned on to a display board. Beforehand, cut an X-shape into the backing card. This will form the hole you poke the bottle through, so make it to fit. Paint the background card in dark blue or black and splatter on stars with white or yellow paint if desired. Make angels using the bottles as the bodies. Fill the bottle with lengths of tinsel, lametta or shredded foil. Draw a face on a paper oval and tape the face flat on top of the neck of the bottle. Add pipe-cleaner wings and a halo. Push the angel's backside through the X in the backing card far enough for it to be safely wedged. Attach thread to the card for hanging.

Talk about
What's it like when heaven breaks through on to earth?

2 Shepherds' hot chocolate

You will need: hot-chocolate powder; mini marshmallows; sprinkles; squirty cream; warm milk (not too hot)

Make hot chocolate drinks with all the extras.

Talk about
The shepherds didn't have drinking chocolate, but if it had been available in those days they might well have been knocking it back around their campfire before the angels came.

3 Sheep sock puppets

You will need: old (clean!) black socks; white felt (cut into two triangles per sheep); googly eyes; PVA glue; spreaders; cotton wool

Make a sheep puppet out of the sock with felt triangles glued on for ears. Attach the googly eyes, then stick the cotton wool on top of the head and on the body.

Talk about
Using the puppets, tell the shepherds' story from the point of view of the sheep.

4 Nativity storyteller

> **You will need:** squares of paper; Christmas story stickers or cut-outs of clip art

Make a 'fortune teller' from the origami pattern to be found online (search for 'origami fortune teller'), or in most school playgrounds. Stick pictures of Mary, Jesus, Gabriel and a shepherd on the innermost fold-out points and put images of the star, a stable, a sheep and Bethlehem on the outside, with numbers in the middle as usual. See how people use them in different ways to tell parts of the Christmas story.

Talk about
How much can you tell me about each person or thing or place in the Christmas story in the model you've made?

5 Cheese candles

> **You will need:** rye biscuits or similar large, rectangular savoury biscuits; packs of square cheese slices; carrots or radishes; cucumber; soft cheese in a tube

Cut a cheese slice in half to make two rectangles and put one on your biscuit, orientated 'portrait', as the candle. Add a carrot chip or half a radish as the flame and decorate the base with circles of cucumber. Squeeze a frame of soft cheese around it.

Talk about
Jesus is the light of the world.

6 Giant paper chains

You will need: rolls of wallpaper; staplers; sturdy cord; spray bottles; runny paint

Many of us have made pretty little paper chains in the past, and this is the same principle, scaled up as large as it will go without breaking under its own weight. You could use the cord to hold it up if you want to cheat. Make a paper chain out of the wallpaper (you could experiment with loops interlocked or with the concertina type). Make it a more cheerful colour if needed by squirting it with runny paint from spray bottles.

Talk about
What you're looking forward to over the Christmas season.

7 Build-and-draw live stable

You will need: props to make a stable scene: straw, guinea pig hay, a manger, sacks, buckets, characters; artists' charcoal; big sheets of good-quality paper

Set up a stable scene and have two people dressed as Mary and Joseph—and a baby if you have a handy one. Invite people to come quietly into the stable and draw what they see. You could have quiet music playing to help the mood. Note: watch out for people with hay fever

Talk about
Tell me about what you've chosen to draw.

8 Cork table decoration

You will need: corks or play dough; old CDs; either craft wire and confetti stars or the tinselly decoration that has stars sticking out from curly wire; big paper clips; PVA glue; spreaders; scissors

Use the paper clip to poke holes in the cork. Stick short lengths of wire into the cork and wind the loose ends round some confetti stars. Have them sticking out wildly in all directions. Glue the cork base on to the CD to hold it upright. An easier version for little ones is for them to cut up the ready-starred wire into short lengths and poke those into the cork or a play-dough base.

Talk about
The wise men followed the star.

9 Frankincense hand rub

You will need: unscented baby oil; a small bottle of essential oil of frankincense, suitable for use on skin; bowl

Mix the baby oil with a few drops of the essential oil in the bowl. After checking for allergies, treat people to a relaxing hand rub with the perfumed baby oil. Enjoy the smell of it.

Talk about
How busy are you in the run-up to Christmas? Would it help if I prayed for you?

10 Gift tags

You will need: good-quality card or old Christmas cards; tag shapes cut on a die-cutting machine or by hand; gift ribbon; decorative stickers, bows, trims and other Christmassy tat; PVA glue; spreaders; scissors

Create a set of gift tags to make your gifts look beautiful.

Talk about
God gave us the gift of Jesus at Christmas time.

CELEBRATION

Are you looking forward to Christmas? It's a busy time and an exciting time, with lots of things to do to get ready.

What things will you be busy doing in your home to get ready? (*Putting up the tree; buying and wrapping presents; putting up cards and decorations; buying special food…*)

We'll be as busy as Martha was when she was getting ready to welcome Jesus—do you remember her and her duster? Let's all have a dust… and a hoover. *Mime dusting and hoovering.*

We're getting ready for special visitors in our house. Has anyone else got family members coming to stay? We need to make the bed for them. Let's all put a clean sheet on the bed together. *Mime putting on a sheet.*

Imagine if we didn't bother—if the guests arrived and there was nowhere ready for them to stay. We could say, 'Sorry, we've no room, but you can put this tent up in the garden if you like, or you can have these blankets and lie down next to the lawnmower and the broken bicycle in the garage.' How do you think they'd feel? (*Left out in the cold? Not welcome, wanted or loved?*)

That's what happened on the very first Christmas night.

Mary and Joseph had had a very long journey all the way to Bethlehem. They must have been hungry and exhausted, and Mary was about to have her baby. But there was nowhere for them to stay. Nobody had dusted for them. Nobody had hoovered. Nobody had made a bed. There was no warm cot for Mary's baby. So Jesus had to sleep in a trough made of wood or perhaps even cold stone, used for feeding animals.

And yet this baby was the most important visitor ever to come to this earth: God's son.

The name Mary and Joseph gave him was Jesus. But in the Bible he has another name too: Immanuel, which means 'God is with us'. Jesus came to be with us, to be part of our human family and to bring us all together in love as God's family.

In all your busy preparations, don't forget to make room for Jesus to be with you in your celebrations. Perhaps you could sing a carol for him when you get up on Christmas morning. Or say a prayer just thanking him for being with you.

Prayer

Let's all stand or sit or kneel round the manger and say the repeated line with me: 'Lord Jesus, come and stay with us.'

Jesus, whose mother was Mary,
we pray for our families, that we may not take each other for granted.
Lord Jesus, come and stay with us.

Jesus, lying in a manger,
we pray for those who don't have anywhere to live. Help them find shelter and helpful friends.
Lord Jesus, come and stay with us.

Jesus, sharing the stable with the animals,
we pray for all of your creation so full of life. Help us to look after the earth you have given us.
Lord Jesus, come and stay with us.

Jesus, worshipped by shepherds and kings,
we pray for all the different countries of the world, for an end to fighting and
wars and unfair situations.
Lord Jesus, come and stay with us.

Jesus, our Immanuel,
we pray for those who are unwell, and ask that you would be with them,
comfort them and help them get better.
Lord Jesus, come and stay with us.

Sunday treat

… the love of God…

God, our Father, your love is so big we can't measure it.
It's too wide, too long, too high, too… **(say your own ideas).**
Nothing can separate us from your love, not even accidents or… **(say your**
own ideas).
You are always with us.

Take-home idea

Each choose your favourite Christmas carol:

✣ Why is this your favourite carol? Is it the tune, the words or something else?
✣ Which part of the Christmas story does it relate to?
✣ Which is your favourite part of the Christmas story?

Messy team theme

✣ Is the picture of God in your head one of God as a tiny baby or a grown-up?
✣ What memory of Christmas in church would you most like your families to go away with?
✣ What present has God given you through your Messy Church?

Session 13

Money matters

HOW DOES THIS SESSION HELP PEOPLE GROW IN CHRIST?

At the time of writing, money is hardly ever out of the news and seems to be mentioned in almost every conversation. It is a major preoccupation for many families, and given that Jesus has plenty to say about money, it is important to offer a Messy Church session on the subject. There are themes of gratitude, stewardship, boundaries, security and counting our blessings. Our attitude to money can be a blessing or a worry.

Main Bible story: Luke 21:1–4

ACTIVITIES

1 Bubble-wrap printing

You will need: 'big' bubble wrap; paint; large sheets of paper (from a lining-paper roll or similar); potato printers cut in the shape of £ $ and other currency symbols (do an internet search on 'worldwide currency symbols'); gold or yellow and black paint in trays

This is a big messy activity! You're printing all the coins in the world. Allow generously sized squares of bubble wrap for each person and lashings of gold or yellow paint. Lay the bubble wrap on the paint, then print so that the paper is covered with gold circles (coins). Then stamp each circle with a currency sign in black paint.

Talk about
What is 'being rich'? Is it about how much money you hold on to or how much money you're able to let go of? Or is it nothing to do with money at all? How much money would it take to make you happy? Do you think you would ever have 'enough'?

2 Charity money box

You will need: card; decorations; scissors; PVA glue; spreaders; details of a charity

Make and then decorate a collecting box for your chosen charity in a shape that reflects that charity's work, if possible. (We made some splendid little toilets from circular yoghurt pots with card lids and seats for the Tearfund Toilet Twinning scheme.) Include a leaflet about the charity and the date by which you want the money back.

Talk about
Enthuse people about the charity's work and how they can make a difference by saving their loose change in the box and bringing it back by a set date. Sharing what we have is one of the best ways to make the world a fairer place.

3 Replica ten-pound note

You will need: copies of ten pound notes with 'SAMPLE' printed across them to avoid misunderstandings; paper; appropriately coloured fine-nib pens

Invite people to make a ten-pound note of their own, copying the pictures or patterns on the original, but writing on it a promise to give not ten pounds but something to someone else. It might be a promise to give a hug, to lend a hand with the washing up, to walk the dog, to give a box of chocolates or something else that isn't money.

Talk about
How hard it is to practise giving rather than getting or grabbing. But Jesus loves it when we give to others.

4 Sharing play dough

You will need: play dough; play-dough tools

Play with play dough and talk about making sure that everyone has enough, about sharing the tools, about how it feels if one person takes it all and someone else has none.

Talk about
The best way to learn about sharing is to do it.

5 Grab game

You will need: plastic coins taped to strings; other plastic coins without strings; a timer; long piece of string

Play in pairs. Player 1 has ten stringed coins in front of them. The loose ends of the strings are within their opponent's reach. Player 2 has just coins in front of them (and the loose ends of string). Lay the long piece of string across the table to be the 'net' between the two players. Set the timer for one minute. Player 1 needs to try to grab the coins on strings as player 2 yanks them away one at a time. Player 1 has to try to KEEP his money. Player 2, as well as yanking the strings, is trying to flick her coins into the other side of the court: she is trying to GIVE AWAY all her money. Player 1 needs to flick them back as soon as they come over to his side. At the end of one minute, player 1 gets a point for each coin on a string on his side and player 2 gets a point for every coin successfully on the other side of the 'net'. Swap over and play again.

Talk about
In the early 19th century, William Wordsworth wrote a sonnet about the madness of grabbing and spending:

> *The world is too much with us; late and soon,*
> *Getting and spending, we lay waste our powers:*
> *Little we see in Nature that is ours;*
> *We have given our hearts away, a sordid boon!*

Does wanting more and more money (getting) or spending ages shopping (spending) stop us enjoying life fully? Or is it the only way to live in a consumer society?

6 DIY display-box collage

> **You will need:** a big box or cylinder (a washing-powder box is ideal); a roll of double-sided sticky film; pictures; shapes; junk-modelling materials; selected phrases from Matthew 6:25–34 (ones that mean something to you) printed out on card

Cover the box or cylinder in double-sided sticky film, so that it both sticks to the box and has a sticky surface. Have a box full of collage pictures and shapes which you could theme on money, cheques, credit cards, shares and similar. People can slap the shapes and photos on to the sticky surface to make a dynamic 3D collage sculpture—dynamic because you can rip bits off and replace them as the sculpture grows.

Talk about

Many people are worried about money. Jesus said wise words about worry in Matthew 6:25–34.

7 Temple treasury pot

You will need: for older people, strips of magazine or newspaper about 5cm x 30cm; jars; elastic bands; for younger people, jars, tubes or cans without sharp edges to decorate; golden scraps; sticky tape; PVA glue; spreaders

Younger people can simply have a happy time making a golden, decorated pot. Older people can weave a pot as follows:

Fold the rough edges of the paper strips in on themselves a couple of times so that they are tucked away inside the strips, which should end up about 2cm wide. Tape two strips across one another in a cross shape. Add two more to make a star shape and tape them all together. The centre of this star will be the base of the pot.

Place the star over something firm like an upturned jar and bend the loose ends down around it, holding them in place with an elastic band. Then turn the jar the right way up. Starting at the base, weave other strips of newspaper in and out of the ends of the star, pulling each one tightly and attaching the ends together with tape as each 'circle' is completed. Leave enough unwoven ends at the top to fold down inside the woven pot. Tape them into place once you have removed the pot from the jar.

Talk about

Describe how there were large containers outside the Temple in Jerusalem, into which people would drop their money as a gift to God. Some people gave lots of money and you could hear it chinking, while others didn't put much in at all.

8 Tiddlywinks

You will need: either counters with £ signs on or small plastic coins; a pot

Play tiddlywinks to get the money in the temple treasury pot.

Talk about
Has there ever been a time when you've given something away?

9 Silent auction

You will need: some form of invented currency; cards with a tempting picture of one of the following on each (or equivalents that suit your families): fast car, powerful motorbike, designer clothes, latest electronic game, cute cuddly toy, box of chocolates, health, family, friends, happy home, education, good job (leave space on the cards for writing); pens

Give each person the same amount of your invented currency, for example, 'ten splongs' or whatever name you've chosen. Explain that there are many wonderful items on display and they can bid for them with their splongs. They simply see what's on offer, then write under the picture on the cards they are interested in how many splongs they are prepared to bid for them.

They might like to keep coming back to see whether they've been outbid and whether they want to put their splongs on other items. At the end of the session you can give the cards to the people who have bid successfully.

Talk about
What is really valuable in life?

10 Coins to eat

You will need: peppermint cream or fondant icing; yellow food colouring; a clean coin with a milled edge or a clean fine-toothed comb; small circular biscuit cutters; cocktail sticks

Roll out the peppermint cream or fondant icing, then use the biscuit cutter to cut out coin shapes. Draw a design using the cocktail stick, then 'mill' the outer edge by rolling it round the edge of the real milled coin, or, if you can't find a coin big enough, use a fine-toothed comb flat-side on to make imprints.

Talk about
What do we do with our pocket money or our spare cash?

CELEBRATION

Today we've been thinking about why Jesus is really pleased with us when we're generous to other people.

Now, I have two chocolate biscuits. Would it be generous if I kept both? Kept one? Kept half of one? Well, I'll tell you what: I'll give away both. How generous is that?

Jesus was watching people putting money into the temple treasury one day. He saw a lot of very rich people who put in a lot of money, and then he noticed a woman who was dressed in very cheap, old clothes. And he saw what she put into the treasury box too. She put in two tiny copper coins. And Jesus said to his friends, 'You know, she's put in more than all the others. They only gave what they could afford, but she gave everything she had to God.'

Let's tell this story together. It's a bit like 'The House that Jack Built', so join in with the actions and the words as soon as you can.

This is the smile of Jesus. **(Sketch out a big smile with a finger.)**

This is the widow humble and poor **(hunch over with hands clasped)**
Who caused the smile of Jesus. **(Repeat the smile gesture and all the gestures in the following verses as they add on to each other.)**

This is the cloth woven all night **(mime folding cloth in your arms)**
By the widow humble and poor
Who caused the smile of Jesus.

These are the two tiny copper coins **(pretend to place two tiny coins on your palm)**
Earned by selling the cloth woven all night…

These are the rich with their handfuls of gold **(act like a proud person bowing to the right and left)**
Who laughed at the two tiny copper coins…

This is the size of the widow's gift **(spread out your arms as wide as possible)**
Compared with the rich with their handfuls of gold…

The widow gave all she had.
(Show a picture of Jesus on the cross.)
Jesus generously gave all he had for us.
How much do we want to give back to him in thanks?

Prayer

You'll need lots of small coins and a large metal pot

Everyone's going to have two small coins each, just as the widow did, not to keep for ourselves but to give away. This will help us to get in practice for giving away some of our money to help others. Lots of

Christians and other people too give away a tenth of all they earn to help others. We're going to collect money for... (*a charity that helps others*). And, more importantly, we're going to pray as we do it; this is the best way of giving.

✛ Drop your coins one at a time into the pot.
✛ As you drop one in, say thank you to God for something he's generously given you.
✛ As you drop in the second, ask God to help someone you know who needs his help.

Sunday treat

... the fellowship of the Holy Spirit...

Holy Spirit of Jesus, we can't see you, but we know you're there.
You move between us as quietly as a..., as invisibly as... **(say your own ideas)**.
You help us love people who are unlovable and you live in each of us, making us more like Jesus.
Be like a brighter light in us. Be like... **(say your own ideas)**.

Take-home idea

This month, try to give away something every Saturday. Ideas include: putting money in a charity collecting box; giving things you no longer need to a charity shop; making a gift or card for someone else; or giving five minutes to help someone in your family.

Messy team theme

✛ How well off is your Messy Church for money?
✛ How are you enriching the families who come to Messy Church?
✛ Is there anything more you would like to offer to Jesus as a team (not just money!)?

Session 14

Pets and peace

HOW DOES THIS SESSION HELP PEOPLE GROW IN CHRIST?

I've included the theme of pets as it acknowledges that what is important to a great many people is important to God too. Pets play a large part in the lives of many families, and owning a pet can have a profound effect on a child as they learn to look after it, form a bond with it and grieve for it when it dies. It raises questions about love, life and death. On this basis, the Church can celebrate what pets bring to a family, ponder existential questions together and explore how much God cares about all parts of his creation. The celebration focuses on the symbolism of animals on God's holy mountain, and the theme of reconciled enemies, as you can find plenty of liturgies on the more obvious choice of the Genesis creation story elsewhere.

You might like to make this a Messy Church to which pets are invited, but I would suggest they only come for the celebration part, as two hours is a long time. Perhaps a normally stay-at-home member of the family could bring them at the appropriate point. The cardinal rule is that all animals must be in cages, locked in baskets or on leads. Alternatively, you could invite everyone to bring or make an animal headdress or mask to wear, or to bring a cuddly toy or a photo of their pet.

Main Bible story: Isaiah 11:1–3; 6–9

ACTIVITIES

1 Animal head finger puppet

You will need: foam balls (styrofoam or similar—home-made blocks of polystyrene work fine); red felt; fabric; googly eyes; felt/funky foam scraps; pipe cleaners; PVA glue; spreaders; scissors

Cut the foam ball in two with a waxed sharp knife before the session starts. Cut out a piece of red felt as wide as the ball's diameter and long enough to fit across the flat sides of the two halves. Glue the felt to both halves (think of a bread roll with a folded piece of ham in the middle). The felt makes the hinge for the puppet and is the inside of its mouth too. Make two dents side by side in the back of the top half for fingers and one for a thumb in the underneath half. Decorate the puppet head with fake fur, fabric, eyes, ears, antennae or whatever your imagination suggests.

Talk about
How does your animal get on with the other puppet animals? Can you imagine them all living together without fighting or eating each other? That's part of what it will be like when God's kingdom is fully realised.

2 Paper strip pets/rock pets/pom-pom pets/ origami pets

You will need: construction paper strips 12cm x 0.5cm in bright colours; rocks or stones; pom-poms; googly eyes; feathers; pipe cleaners; origami paper; scissors; PVA glue; spreaders; acrylic paint

Older people may enjoy making a precision-built paper strip creature or an origami one, while younger people might prefer to make a basic rock or pom-pom pet by gluing eyes on and adding paint or feathers. For the strip creature, invite people to loop and fold the strips of construction paper ingeniously to make a simple 3D animal. Then they can add paws, feet, ears and eyes. Origami penguins are quite easy and seriously sweet; find instructions online.

Talk about

There is a huge variety of different creatures in the world. Which are your favourites? What do you think God's favourite animal might be? Why?

3 Plastic-bag aquarium

You will need: cheap hair gel—blue, green or clear; self-sealing plastic bags; assorted foam shapes; foil wrapping paper; plastic packet offcuts or anything that can be cut into a fish or coral shape and won't dissolve; fish templates; pens; scissors; stapler; sticky tape; paper plates; cellophane

Cut out several fish shapes, including sharks, sea monsters or piranhas as desired, from the materials on offer. Cut out some weeds or coral. You could simply pop everything in the self-sealing bag with some hair gel and let it all be free-floating, then zip it shut and squash it, or you could tape the weeds/coral to the inside of the bag and just have the fish being mobile in the gel. If the budget doesn't run to hair gel, you can make a good aquarium by cutting the centres out of two paper plates, covering the resulting space with clear plastic from packaging, sticking the fish shapes on to the clear plastic of one plate, then sandwiching the fish between the two plates and stapling the plates together.

Talk about

Swimming and keeping fish. What happens when they die? You might like to think beforehand about the 'Will my fish go to heaven?' question.

4 Pet on a string

You will need: card; plastic strips roughly 15cm x 2cm, cut from a milk carton or similar; corks; string; drawing pins, map tacks or paper clips; sticks (optional); pens; scissors

Make a slit in one end of the cork beforehand with a sharp knife. Without including the tail, draw and colour in a fat pet shape on the card (for example, a bird, a dog, a cat, a rabbit or indeed a dinosaur). Cut it out. Take the plastic strip and fold it in half widthways. Then fold each end diagonally to one side to make the two 'fans' for the propeller or tail. Push a drawing pin (or a map tack, or a paperclip that you've unwound and twisted at one end to make a non-pointy end) through the halfway crease in the plastic strip and then into the slit-free end of the cork. Push the cardboard animal's backside into the slit in the cork (see diagram, page 188). Punch a hole in the animal's head, thread a string through and attach it to a stick if using (you might have a health-and-safety issue with certain people and sticks). Hold it up and run with your pet's tail whirling behind you.

Talk about

We need to look after our pets and exercise them. We need to care for the whole planet as well as our own pets.

5 Falling sparrows

You will need: old gloves or cheap surgical gloves; pennies; brown pom-poms; googly eyes; felt scraps; scissors; PVA glue

Jesus said, 'Are not five sparrows sold for two pennies? Yet not one of them is forgotten by God... Don't be afraid; you are worth more than many sparrows' (Luke 12:6–7). Make a sparrow by gluing two eyes and a felt beak to a brown pom-pom, then glue the sparrow to one finger of the glove so that it sits as if on God's finger when you put the glove on. Make another four of these sparrows, gluing each one on a finger of the glove and glue two pennies into the palm of the glove.

Talk about

How do you think God remembers to care for every single sparrow in the world? How do you think he remembers to care for every single person in the world? Do you ever feel 'forgotten' by God?

6 Dinosaur roarer

You will need: plastic cups; short lengths of wood, for example, disabled matchsticks or lolly stick halves; string at least 1m long; water; a sharp, pointy tool to make holes in cups

Make a hole in the base of the cup and thread the string through. Secure one end inside the cup either with a knot or more securely by tying the string around the matchstick or lolly stick half. Wet the string and run your fingers down it—it makes an impressive dinosaur noise. Experiment with different lengths of string.

Talk about

Can you imagine something as ferocious as a Tyrannosaurus rex cuddling up to your pet rabbit, like in the Isaiah passage? That's how different God's kingdom is from what we're used to on Planet Earth at the moment.

7 Big picture

You will need: either animal pictures from magazines or paint and brushes to paint your own; scissors; PVA glue; spreaders; paper

Encourage people to imagine what God's holy mountain might look like before creating their artwork. Don't be limited to the animals mentioned in the passage, but include animals that are significant to the people present: for example, the goldfish will swim happily with the shark and the hamster will be friends with the cat.

Talk about

What a wonderful world we live in, and how much more wonderful God wants it to be—a place where everyone and everything can feel safe.

8 Endangered animals treasure hunt

You will need: envelopes; PVA glue; spreaders; sets of printed pictures of endangered species like polar bears, parrots, orang-utans, white rhinos, sea turtles, Goliath frogs (Wikipedia has a long list under 'endangered species'); a big picture of a mountain with water near it

Hide envelopes full of pictures of each animal around your building, with a picture of the animal glued to the outside of the envelope. Invite people to go and search for the endangered species and to bring back a picture of each one to put on the holy mountain where everything is safe.

Talk about

How can we care for the planet and its species—especially ones that we're keen on?

9 Interchangeable animals

You will need: card; templates; pens; scissors; crayons

Make some basic animal/fish/bird body shapes, large, medium and small. They should all have two slots for legs to fit into. Make some basic leg shapes that will fit into the slots of the body shapes and hold them upright. Include short, medium and long ones with different hooves/paws/fins on the end. These can all be very simple and stylised. People could either just play with your shapes, colouring them in and fitting them together in many hilarious combinations, or they could construct their own set to take home. A version of this for younger children is to have cards on which a head, body or tail is drawn. Make several sets that can be fitted together in different combinations.

Talk about

Naming the creatures you've made (hipporaffe, crocofrog and so on). Why do you think God gave Adam the job of naming the animals at the start of the world?

10 Badge

You will need: discs of card printed with a border saying 'God animals humans'; safety pins; funky foam, felt, googly eyes; animal print fabric; card or foam; scissors; PVA glue; spreaders; sticky tape

Make an animal badge to wear. Simple, strong designs work best with distinctive animals like pigs, rabbits, elephants, cats or crocodiles.

Talk about
Discuss the words in the border of the badge. At Messy Church today we're thinking about the way God cares for the whole of his creation, including the animals and including us.

CELEBRATION

We've got a lot of animals here today. We've got to be careful though! What do you think would happen if we put this dog and this cat together? Or this cat and this hamster? Or a lion and an antelope? Some creatures are enemies to each other. But that's not how God wanted the world to be, and that's not how it will be one day, when Jesus will make all enemies into friends.

Some books of the Bible were written hundreds of years before Jesus was born. But these books all still point to him. One book was written by the prophet Isaiah. Isaiah listened to what God told him and saw what God showed him and wrote it down so that we could know how God was going to make enemies into friends.

God showed Isaiah someone very special who would come to earth to make enemies into friends. 'One day,' he told Isaiah, 'I will send somebody who will be so wise and powerful and full of godliness that he'll turn everything back to front! All the things that are wrong in the world, he'll put right. All the enemies who hate each other will be friends too, because of his power to change people.'

Isaiah couldn't get his head round someone so amazing, so God showed him a picture of a beautiful mountain—a mountain with a big surprise. 'Imagine a world like this!' God said to Isaiah. 'Look! The animals are all living together in peace with human beings. Let's see if we can tell what animals God showed Isaiah.

For every creature in bold type, display a picture for people to identify.

173

Try to find pictures that make the predators look as savage as possible and the prey as vulnerable as possible.

> The **wolf** will live with the **lamb**,
> the **leopard** will lie down with the **goat**,
> the **calf** and the **lion** together;
> and a little child will lead them.
> The **cow** will feed with the **bear**,
> **calves** and **bear cubs** will lie down together,
> and the **lion** will eat straw like the **ox**.
> Children will play near the hole of the **cobra**;
> Children will put their hands into the **rattlesnake's** nest.
> They will neither harm nor destroy
> on all my holy mountain.

What an amazing person Jesus is, to make enemies like these into friends!

Prayer

You will need a large cross either lying or drawn on the ground; two baskets full of plastic animals (for example, farm animals, zoo animals or dinosaurs)—one with predators and one with prey.

Choose a 'fierce' animal and a 'docile' animal and hold on to them for a moment while we pray together:

Jesus, thank you that you came to turn enemies into friends. Thank you for the world full of animals for us to enjoy. Help us to be their friends and not their enemies and to look after them. Help us to listen to you like Isaiah did and find the way to be friends with our enemies.

Now place your two animals on the cross and say thank you to Jesus for the way his cross makes enemies into friends.

Sunday treat

… Father, Son and Holy Spirit…

God the Father, Jesus the Son and the Holy Spirit, you are three and one God all at the same time!
*This is as mysterious as a Sherlock Holmes adventure, or the way spiders make webs or… **(say your own ideas)**.*

Take-home idea

Find out which animals everyone in the family loves best and which ones you find the scariest. This month, try to help each other make friends with the scary ones: try watching a spider weave a web or try visiting a zoo and admiring the way snakes wiggle. If you can't shed your fear of them (and I'm really not good with spiders myself), find one thing about them to thank God for.

Messy team theme

✛ Share one lesson you learned from an animal.
✛ Is your Messy Church team most like a zoo, a farm, the savannah or a jungle?
✛ What aspect of peace is most needed in your community?

Session 15

Healthy body, healthy soul

HOW DOES THIS SESSION
HELP PEOPLE GROW IN CHRIST?

It's obvious that 'life in all its fullness' is going to feature wholeness and healing; health of body and soul; physical well-being and spiritual peace of mind; a balanced life. Health is a sign of the kingdom. We're given plenty of advice about healthy eating and exercise, but the church needs to show that things of the body are important to God, as are things of the soul. Seeing your Messy Church as a body, with everyone having a different part to play, could also give people a sense of connectedness and significance, help them celebrate differences and give them a reason for loving their neighbours.

Main Bible story: 1 Corinthians 12:12–27

ACTIVITIES

1 Pea-planting for peace

You will need: sweet pea or edible pea seeds; compost; tiny pots or cardboard egg cartons; plant labels or lolly sticks; water

Plant the seeds and water them. Then write, 'Live at peas with everyone' (Romans 12:18) on a plant label or lolly stick and stick it in the soil. How you'll laugh.

Talk about

How God loves it when people find ways of making peace with each other. What can you do to keep the peace at home/school/work? Is your life full of peace at the moment? When your pea plant grows, let it remind you of how important it is to be a peacemaker.

2 Rainbow body

You will need: outlines of people shapes—the hole left after cutting out a person shape (for example, the offcut from a die-cutting machine); tissue paper or cellophane in different colours (sweet wrappers could be used); PVA glue; spreaders; scissors

Stick strips of tissue paper or cellophane or sweet wrappers over the person-shaped space to make a 'stained-glass window' effect.

Talk about

If the person stands for your class at school or your team at work, and every colour of paper or cellophane stands for something different about the people in it, what sort of things are different about the people in that group? Do the colours work well together in your artwork? What would it be like if all the strips were the same colour?

3 Broken-heart fridge magnet

You will need: strips of magnetic tape; a heart template about 5cm high; stiff card; wax crayons; printed messages on paper; PVA glue; spreaders; scissors

Use the template to draw a heart on the stiff card, then cut it out. Colour it in and glue on the message 'Be at peace with each other'

(Mark 9:50). Cut it in two with a jagged break and stick a magnetic strip on the back of each half.

Talk about
When things go wrong in our family, we can each take half of the heart as a way of saying that we're very sad and our heart is breaking. Then we can stick them back together again to say sorry and to make friends with each other.

4 Mouse mat

You will need: sheets of funky foam large enough to make a circle 20cm in diameter, either with or without a self-adhesive side; circular template (or plate) 20cm in diameter; magazine pictures on thick, glossy paper; transparent book-covering film; gel pens or thick felt-tip pens; PVA glue; spreaders

Draw a circle on the foam using the template and cut it out. Do the same with the magazine pictures and the book-covering film. On the picture in a contrasting colour pen write, 'Hold on to what is good, reject whatever is harmful' (1 Thessalonians 5:21–22). Stick the film over the picture and the picture to the foam.

Talk about
It's easy to find wonderful things on the internet, and to find harmful things on it too. God wants us to focus on things that are good for us and help us grow in healthy ways. Your mouse mat can remind you to keep your mind safe as you explore online.

5 Exercise balloon bags

You will need: un-inflated balloons; rice; funnels; sticky tape

This activity is more suited to older people. Choose two balloons in different colours for your ball and cut the necks off them. Blow up a third balloon and keep it blown up for half a minute, then let the air out and put the funnel in its neck. Pour in enough rice to fit comfortably in the palm of a hand. Take the funnel out and cut off the hard ring on the neck of that balloon, then fold the neck back against the side of the balloon and tape it into place. Carefully stretch one of the first two balloons over the filled balloon. Carefully pull the other balloon over the ball and it's ready to play with.

Talk about
How could you use this ball to exercise? (For example, to make your fingers and thumbs or wrists strong, or by throwing to improve hand-eye coordination.) Do you think God is bothered if we don't treat our bodies well and keep them in good order? Why, or why not? What do you think Paul means in his letter when he says, 'Do you not know that your bodies are temples of the Holy Spirit, who is in you?' (1 Corinthians 6:19).

6 Mini-marshmallow sculpture

You will need: lots and lots of mini-marshmallows; lots and lots of cocktail sticks

Build sculptures using the two materials. See how well they join together. Eat the results. (You may want to combine this with a make-your-own-toothpaste activity: mix three parts bicarbonate of soda with one part salt, enough glycerine to make a firm paste and a drop of flavouring, for example, peppermint oil.)

Talk about
How are we connected to other people? Through friendships, family ties, Facebook, Skype or email, as well as through playing with them and spending time with them face to face. A body would look very

silly if it was all separate body parts: they need to be joined together, like these sculptures. How can we be better joined together in our church or in our family?

7 Tessellating shapes plaque

You will need: tessellating shapes (rectangles, squares, equilateral triangles or hexagons)—ready-cut for younger ones, but older people can use a template and cut their own out of scrapbook paper; wallpaper samples or comic/magazine pages; scissors; PVA glue; spreaders; large sheets of card; metallic pens

Try to arrange the shapes on a big piece of card so that there are no gaps between them. Adjust them until they make a design you are satisfied with, then glue them in place, leaving a border round the edge, where you could write in metallic pen 'In Jesus you are being built together' (Ephesians 2:22).

Talk about
What makes it difficult to fit together with other people as well as these shapes fit together with each other? When have you known a time on TV or in a book or in your own life when a group of people—friends or family or others—fitted together really well?

8 Recycled hat

You will need: old stretchy sweatshirts; fabric scissors; adult supervision

Cut the sleeve off an old sweatshirt and remove the cuff. From the cuff end, cut slits up the sleeve, about 15cm long. Randomly tie some of these strips together in double knots and leave a few dangling. Roll up the shoulder end of the sleeve and wear on your head with pride.

Talk about
How do we decorate our bodies? How important are clothes, shoes, jewellery, tattoos and piercings?

9 Balloon-powered cars

You will need: tissue boxes or similar; plastic straws; wooden kebab sticks; lids or CDs for wheels; balloons; scissors

Cut the box into an open-top car shape (precision and classiness aren't important—you just need to make a chassis of some sort). Make two holes in each side (ensuring that they line up), push the kebab sticks through the straws and push them through the holes in the chassis to make the axles. Make holes in the centre of the lids to make the wheels and push the ends of the kebab sticks into them. Make a hole in the back of the car and carefully push the end of a blown-up balloon through it. See how far and fast it powers the car.

Talk about
It's very doubtful that you'll have the chance to talk about anything but speed, but you might be able to say something about what gives our bodies energy to move and what the breath of God's Spirit can do to energise us.

10 Big body

You will need: junk-modelling materials; sticky tape; lengths of tubing; bags; foam; old clockwork or mechanisms

Make a big body out of the junk. Can you make any 'working parts'? (You might want to censor this mildly if teenagers get going on it.) A pumping heart? A filtering kidney? Eyeballs that swivel? Knees that bend?

Talk about
Our bodies are indeed 'fearfully and wonderfully made' (Psalm 139:14). Which parts do you find the most amazing? Which would you be most proud of if you had designed it?

CELEBRATION

If possible, tape the outline of a body shape on the floor with masking tape, large enough to fit everyone inside it.

Have a 'shake-out' mini-aerobics session, calling out different parts of the body to shake or wave or bend, and keep up a running commentary of how marvellous each part is. For example:

Let's all get our arms and elbows and hands wiggling. Wow, they are really amazing, aren't they? Think of all the things you can do with your arms *(keep them wiggling!)*. You can reach for things *(let's all reach out)*. You can grab things with your hands *(grab)*. You can hold hands with someone *(hold hands)* or hug them *(hug!)*. You can bend your elbows to get your hands near you *(bend)* and straighten them out again so they're strong enough to lift things up *(mime lifting)*, but you can still scratch your nose *(scratch away)*. And noses! Aren't noses brilliant? and so on.

In the Bible, there's a letter written to some Christians in a church, where the writer tells them that they are so amazing, they're like a body where all the different parts work together really well. They all do different things, and that's really important: imagine what you would look like if you were just one big eye! How would you hear anything? Or if you were just one big ear, how would you smell anything? God made each of us to be different and very, very special to each other. We all have different jobs to do at home and in school or work and in our Messy Church here.

Then find some volunteers. These will be unique to you, but you might say something like this:

Here's John: he's always busy in the kitchen making our tea, so he's like the hands, always chopping and stirring and serving food. Here's Jan: she's really good at listening to people's problems, so she's like an ear. Here's Stephen and he's a great sax player, so he's like a mouth. Elisabeth is on the planning team, so she's a bit like a digestive system, processing nutrients for the rest of us as she decides what things we're going to make and do. Paul helps clear up afterwards, so he's like white blood cells fighting infection and clearing away germs in our systems.

I wonder which part of the body you are most like? Talk to the person you've come with and decide. Then come and stand in this space here where we've marked out a body. As you go and stand in the place that matches your chosen body part, call out your name, what you are and why. For example, 'I'm Ben and I'm good at eating, so I'm a tummy!'

When everyone is positioned, say how amazing it is that every single person is a vital part of the body that God wants us to be— Jesus' body here on earth, doing wonderful things for him and for other people. Get everyone to pat each other on the back and say, 'I need you!'

Prayer

Move out into a circle, or several circles if there are a lot of you. One person holds a ball of wool and calls out, 'Thank you, God, for Tom.' They then throw the ball of wool to Tom, but hold on to the end, so that the first strand of a 'web' stretches across the circle. Tom does the same: 'Thank you, God, for Nora!' Then he throws the ball of wool to Nora but holds onto the strand. Carry on until everyone in the circle has been included and all are holding the wool. The web should be stretched in a haphazard way across the circle. Finish with a prayer that brings all the prayers together with thanks for being a family linked together with the other congregations of your church, with other Messy Churches and with God through Jesus.

Sunday treat

… world without end.

God, there are many scary things around us and we never know what the future will be.
The things that worry us are… (say your own ideas).
But we trust that we belong to your family and that we are part of your world, which will never pass away, but will go on getting better and better for ever and ever.

Take-home idea

Talk about the different things you're good at. Celebrate them by drawing your family on a poster, where all the great things you can do could be written or drawn around you. Thank Jesus for the way he's made you into a unique 'you' and that he loves you just as you are.

Messy team theme

✣ How is our team like a well-functioning body?
✣ No body is perfect this side of heaven. Are there any dysfunctional bits of our team we could change for the better—not by losing people, but by changing the way we relate to each other?
✣ In what ways do we make it easy for people to join us?

Catapult (p. 83)

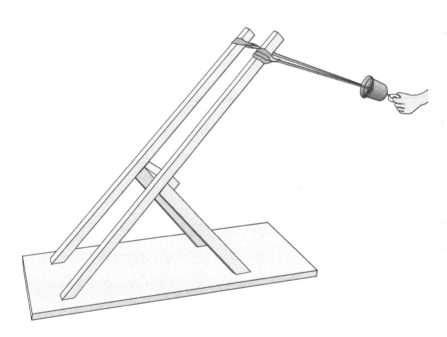

Wind-up boat (p. 112)

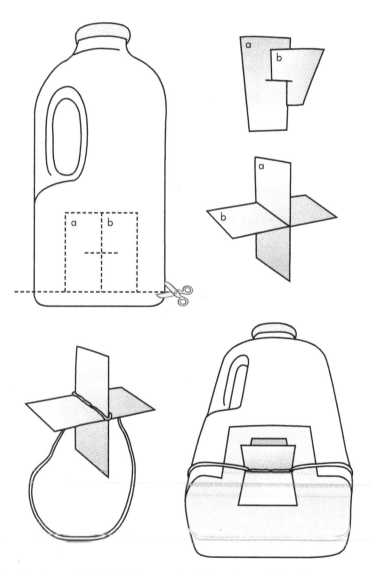

String art frame (p. 139)

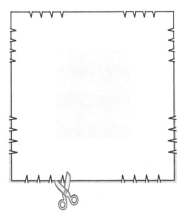

Pet on a string (p. 169)

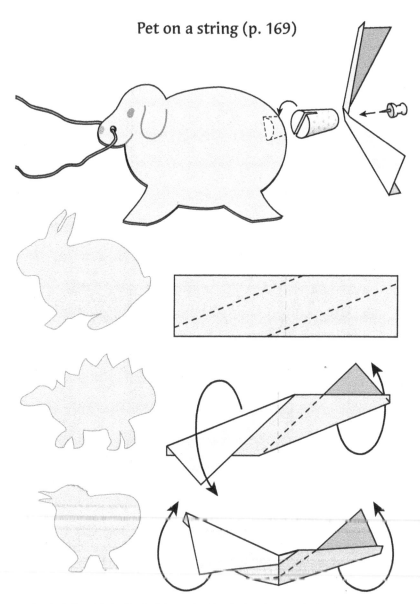

Index of activities

Enjoyed
this book?

Write a review—we'd love to hear what you think.
Email: reviews@brf.org.uk

Keep up to date—receive details of our new books as they happen.
Sign up for email news and select your interest groups at:
www.brfonline.org.uk/findoutmore/

Follow us on Twitter @brfonline

By post—to receive new title information by post (UK only), complete the form below and post to: BRF Mailing Lists, 15 The Chambers, Vineyard, Abingdon, Oxfordshire, OX14 3FE

Your Details
Name
Address
Town/City _____ Post Code _____
Email

Your Interest Groups (*Please tick as appropriate)	
☐ Advent/Lent	☐ Messy Church
☐ Bible Reading & Study	☐ Pastoral
☐ Children's Books	☐ Prayer & Spirituality
☐ Discipleship	☐ Resources for Children's Church
☐ Leadership	☐ Resources for Schools

Support your local bookshop
Ask about their new title information schemes.